FITNESS
WALKING
FOR
WOMEN

Other books by James M. Rippe, M.D.

The Sports Performance Factors (with William Southmayd, M.D.)

Fitness Walking (with Robert Sweetgall and Frank Katch, Ed.D., with John Dignam)

Manual of Cardiovascular Diagnosis and Therapy (with Joseph S. Alpert)

Manual of Intensive Care (with Marie Csete)

Intensive Care Medicine (with R. J. Irwin, J. S. Alpert, and J. E. Dalen)

FITNESS WALKING FOR WOMEN

Anne Kashiwa
&
James M. Rippe, M.D.

A Perigee Book

Perigee Books
are published by
The Putnam Publishing Group
200 Madison Avenue
New York, NY 10016

Library of Congress Cataloging-in-Publication Data

Kashiwa, Anne.
Fitness walking for women.

"A Perigee book."
Includes index.
1. Walking—Physiological aspects. 2. Physical
fitness for women. I. Rippe, James M. II. Title.
RA781.65.K37   1987   613.7'1   87-12749
ISBN 0-399-51407-4

Printed in the United States of America
3   4   5   6   7   8   9   10

To Hank, Hennie and Carol

Acknowledgments

A book of this magnitude requires the efforts and expertise of many individuals. We have drawn support, encouragement and inspiration from many people.

Many of our colleagues at the Exercise Physiology Laboratory at the University of Massachusetts Medical School and the Department of Exercise Science at U/Mass Amherst provided important insights and helped throughout all phases of the manuscript preparation.

Dr. Ann Ward, who is an exercise physiologist and the Research Director of the Exercise Physiology Laboratory at U/Mass Medical School, wrote the chapter on Walking and Weight Loss and also contributed a number of important insights and comments on the entire manuscript. She also played a very central role in a number of the research projects reported in this manuscript.

Dr. Patty Freedson, who is an exercise physiologist and faculty member of the Department of Exercise Science at U/Mass Amherst, wrote an excellent chapter on Muscular Strength and Endurance and co-authored the chapter on Walking for Older Women. In addition, Professor Freedson was a central member at all phases of manuscript preparation and offered numerous helpful comments. She played an essential role in many of the research projects reported in this manuscript.

In addition, fine work was accomplished by Professor Kevin Campbell of the Cleveland Clinic Foundation and Professor Robert Andres of the Biomechanics Lab at U/Mass Amherst, who helped us clarify our thoughts on the walking motion and the role of walking shoes to help Fitness Walkers.

Roxanne Kapitan, B.S., who contributed the chapter on Nutrition, is the Director of Nutriworks, a company that provides corporations with employee nutrition programs. An education specialist, she also trains other health professionals to provide consumers with quality nutrition education programs.

Jan Reynolds, who wrote the chapter on Adventure Walking, is a noted explorer and author. Her treks have included walking trips around the Himalayas, through the African Sahara, and many other places. Her articles have appeared in *The National Geographic*, *The Walking Magazine* and in numerous other publications.

Kim Bertagnoli, M.S., who co-authored the chapter on Walking and Pregnancy, is an exercise physiologist with a special interest in the cardiovascular response to exercise during pregnancy.

Other members of our exercise physiology laboratory who performed excellent work on this project and the many research projects that led up to it include: Dr. Jessica Ross, Sharon Wilkie, Stephanie O'Hanley, Kim Bertagnoli, John Porcari, Greg Kline, Nancy Clark, Robert Hintermeister, Greg Walcott, Sandy Hsieh, Betsy Keller, Dr. Bob McCarron, David Kalmes, Betsy Crawford, Carol Trask, Judy Kleinerman, Rob Coleman and Mike McVeigh.

Special thanks are due to our many friends at The Rockport Company, who offered support for both of us throughout the preparation of this manuscript. Much of the research over the last few years that enabled us to gather the information that we report received support from Rockport. Bruce Katz, Chairman of The Rockport Company, demonstrated commitment and vision to get America walking. Stanley Kravetz, President of The Rockport Company, has continued to support research and education in walking. Beverly Daane, Vice President of Marketing at Rockport, has helped us throughout our work. Alex Hofstetter has also offered valuable help and ideas. To list the many individuals by name at The Rockport Company who have helped us is impossible but our gratitude to them all is very real. However, some to whom we would like to give special thanks include Robert Infantino, Saul and Dorothy Katz, Tony Post, Lisa Harsip, Lynn Gruber, Janice McKeown and Gordon Garvey.

A special word of thanks is due to Carol Cone, President of Cone Communications in Boston, whose early commitment to the walking movement really fostered its growth.

The staff at *The Walking Magazine* helped us clarify our thinking on many issues. Norman Raben, founder and President of Raben Publishing, was particularly helpful in this regard. Craig Woods, former editor of *The Walking Magazine*, and Brad Ketchum, its current editor, and Sue Levin, the articles editor, have been valued friends and allies.

Special inspiration came from our friend and colleague Rob Sweetgall, whose courageous 11,208-mile walk through every state in the United States was a truly pivotal event to get America walking.

Managing our busy professional lives required considerable juggling, where we were greatly aided by our staffs. Beth Porcaro, Dr. Rippe's editorial assistant, played a central role in managing every phase of this manuscript. Mary Ann Falvey, Dr. Rippe's administrative assistant, played a central role in managing all of the details of a busy cardiology practice.

We would particularly like to thank and extend appreciation to Joseph L. Barrow, Jr., of Denver, Colorado, who exhibited great foresight and help to Anne throughout all of her career in walking and for his continued encouragement, sensitivity and endless enthusiasm.

A special word of thanks is due to Daniel Delaney, Anne's father, who has inspired and encouraged her both to be physically active and to write this book. He also helped in the final editing process.

We are especially grateful to our editor, Adrienne Ingrum, who has supported our efforts in preparing this manuscript. Adrienne was one of the earliest advocates of the walking movement who took the courageous step of publishing our first book, *Fitness Walking*, far before anyone else in the publishing industry recognized the potential for walking for fitness.

Finally, once again to Carol Cone, Hank Kashiwa, Hennie Kashiwa, whose endless love makes all of this worthwhile.

Contents

1. Why Should Women Walk?   13
2. Getting Started   25
3. Testing Yourself for Fitness Walking   57
4. Fitness Walking Programs for Women   65
5. Walking and Weight Loss   73
6. Nutrition for the Woman Fitness Walker   79
7. Muscular Strength and Endurance   101
8. Walking for Older Women   107
9. Walking and Pregnancy   111
10. Walking for Rehabilitation   123
11. Racewalking   131
12. Adventure Walking   137

Appendix: Personal Walking Log   146
References   149
Index   152

A daily fitness walk will improve your health, vigor and outlook on life. *Photo: David Brownell*

1
Why Should Women Walk?

This book has a simple premise: making walking a regular part of your life is the easiest, most important thing you can do to keep your heart strong, control your weight and feel vigorous and good. In the following chapters, you'll find all the tools for attaining these goals except one: *motivation.* That comes from you—from your belief that your goals are within your reach. If you're skeptical about walking or if you're not sure you can fit it into your life, read on. You'll be convinced.

Why is this a book on walking for *women?* Because while walking is an ideal activity for everyone, women do have special fitness goals, needs and concerns. Many women need an activity that fits into a busy schedule; others need an effective form of weight control; still others need a simple outlet for stress. Unfortunately, while more women are athletic now than ever before, there are still many women who missed out on the fitness boom. These women, who may have been inactive much of their lives, are attracted to walking for its simplicity and relative gentleness. And many of those younger athletes are tiring of the pounding that comes from running and aerobics—walking offers a sane alternative.

If you consider all of these reasons together, the common denominator is health. Yet many women don't have the complete knowledge of the facts necessary to get the most out of their fitness walking programs. Even the most well-intentioned fitness walkers are sometimes confused about the basics, and as a result, cheat themselves of many of the benefits of exercise.

Making matters worse, a lot of misinformation has been generated by the recent surge in the popularity of walking. This book aims to correct these misconceptions and provide a single, concise statement on the techniques and benefits of fitness walking.

WHAT ARE THE MAJOR HEALTH BENEFITS OF FITNESS WALKING?

The health benefits of fitness walking extend to virtually every body system. Let's list some of the major ones:

- HEART: Fitness walking improves both the strength and efficiency of the heart muscle. In addition, a consistent, lifelong program can decrease your risk of heart attack;
- MUSCLES AND JOINTS: Fitness walking will improve muscular strength and tone the leg muscles as well as strengthen ligaments, tendons and cartilage;
- METABOLISM: Regular walking improves the way the body handles sugar; many diabetics can reduce the amount of insulin they require by starting a fitness walking program;
- BONE STRENGTH: Regular weight-bearing activity such as walking appears to strengthen bones in young women and may retard the process of osteoporosis, which frequently accompanies aging;
- WEIGHT LOSS: Fitness walking is a wonderful and vastly underrated component of an overall plan for weight loss; most important, walking has been shown to preserve lean muscle mass while helping people lose *fat*;
- MENTAL BENEFITS: Regular exercise improves self-image and helps decrease depression and anxiety.

This is only a partial list of the health benefits of fitness walking. Many of them are so important that they have been given entire chapters.

SHORT-TERM CONDITIONING VERSUS LIFELONG HEALTH

The fitness "boom" of the 1970's and early 1980's brought with it varied good concepts and ideas—many of them reaching women for the first time. Many began to exercise regularly, pay attention to their daily health habits and think carefully about nutrition. However, the fitness boom also brought some confusion and misconceptions that have been difficult to break.

Perhaps the area of greatest confusion has been the distinction between short-term "training" or "conditioning" benefits of regular exercise, and the *health* benefits of lifelong regular exercise.

SHORT-TERM "TRAINING" BENEFITS

Many studies have shown that when previously inactive people begin to exercise, a number of changes occur within eight to twelve weeks. These changes include a fall in resting heart rate, an increase in the maximum amount of work they can perform, and the ability to accomplish tasks with less fatigue. In other words, they got in shape. To the exercise physiologist or cardiologist, these changes are called "the training effect," and they indicate that both the heart and muscles do their jobs more efficiently.

The heart's task is to pump out oxygenated blood to the exercising muscles. After eight to twelve weeks of training it pumps more blood with every beat. The muscles then use the oxygen in the blood to convert food energy to a form of energy that allows them to work. After eight to twelve weeks of training they do this more efficiently.

To get this training effect, exercise must be of *sufficient intensity*. According to the American College of Sports Medicine Guidelines, sufficient intensity for the previously inactive person means exercising three times a week for twenty to thirty minutes a session, employing rhythmic exercises that raise the heart rate to 60 to 80 percent of predicted maximum heart rate (the "target training" zone).

Fitness walking is an excellent aerobic training exercise. In the Exercise Physiology Laboratory at the University of Massachusetts Medical School, in studies of over two hundred women, fitness walking raised the heart rate into the target training zone in over 90 percent of individuals. This was true irrespective of age or physical condition.

There is a much more important point to be made, however. Don't confuse short-term training benefits with long-term health benefits. Fitness walking is an excellent exercise to help you achieve your short-term fitness goals, but the area where fitness walking really shines is in long-term health benefits.

LIFELONG HEALTH AND FITNESS WALKING

It's plain fact: exercise increases the quality of life, and recent studies suggest that people who exercise live longer. Over forty studies have been done in the last twenty-five years looking at the relationship between exercise and health, and the findings have been surprisingly consistent: to achieve the most important cardiac *health* benefits from exercise, the exercise must be *consistent* and *lifelong*. Cardiac *health* benefits mean, specifically, the reduction of coronary artery disease—the disease that causes angina and heart attack. The studies have consistently shown that exercise on a regular basis throughout a lifetime will reduce the likelihood of heart attack.

Perhaps the best known recent study to look at the relationship between exercise and heart disease was conducted by Dr. Ralph Paffenbarger and his colleagues. The study, called the College Alumni Study, followed the health habits of over sixteen thousand Harvard graduates for over twenty years. The subjects happened to be all men; however, the findings are just as relevant to women.

What this study showed was that individuals who exercised consistently throughout their lives were significantly less likely to suffer from heart attacks or die from a heart attack than were their less active colleagues.

What form of exercise was most commonly reported? You guessed it—walking. The intensity of the walking was not specifically examined. However, the distances were not very long. People who walked as little as five city blocks a day or climbed five flights of stairs daily achieved significant reduction in heart attacks, and the benefits increased the more they walked. The investigators concluded that people would significantly improve their cardiac health by walking nine miles a week throughout their lives.

While many other activities offer training benefits, few can match walking—which has such a low injury potential and is such a pleasurable activity—in terms of lifelong consistency; and that's the key to how exercise relates to cardiac health.

WALKING AND CARDIAC RISK FACTORS

Don't get it wrong. Exercise is not a cure-all to prevent heart disease. Coronary artery disease is a complex disorder with many contributing causes, also known as risk factors.

Many studies have shed light on the risk factors for coronary artery disease; perhaps the most famous of these is the Framingham Heart Study. Over five thousand citizens of the town of Framingham, Massachusetts, have been followed for over twenty-five years to see how various factors relate to the likelihood of heart disease.

This study has established three major risk factors for coronary artery disease: cigarette smoking, elevated blood cholesterol, and high blood pressure. Other minor risk factors include: diabetes, an inactive lifestyle, a family history of coronary artery disease, stress and obesity.

Cardiac Risk Factors

Major Risk Factors	*Minor Risk Factors*
1. Cigarette smoking	1. Inactive lifestyle
2. Elevated blood cholesterol	2. Family history of coronary artery disease
3. High blood pressure	3. Diabetes
	4. Stress
	5. Obesity

The only risk factor that fitness walking *directly* influences is that of inactive lifestyle; however, it may carry some *indirect* benefits on other cardiac risk factors. You need to pay attention to *all* of the risk factors in order to minimize your risk of coronary artery disease, but here is how your fitness walking program may help.

FITNESS WALKING AND CHOLESTEROL

A very important thing you can do for your heart is to lower the amount of cholesterol in your diet. The major ways to do this are limiting the amount of red meat in your diet (no more than two servings a week), reducing the number of eggs (no more than two a week), switching to low-fat dairy products and being careful about the amount of cheese and ice cream. Regular fitness walking probably will not reduce the total amount of cholesterol in your blood, but it may increase the high density lipoprotein (HDL) fraction of cholesterol. This HDL fraction appears to have some *protective* effect on lowering coronary artery disease.

FITNESS WALKING AND CIGARETTE SMOKING

The U.S. Surgeon General has identified cigarette smoking as the single most important cause of preventable disease and premature death. If you smoke more than a pack of cigarettes a day you increase your likelihood of heart disease by three times and your likelihood of lung cancer by thirty times. Furthermore, risk increases with the amount and duration you smoke. Only quitting can break the pattern and result in a decreased risk of death from heart disease and cancer. One year after you kick the habit, your risk of heart disease declines by approximately 50 percent, and, after ten years, is comparable to that of a person who never smoked.

Another reason to quit is that by smoking you may be endangering the health of those around you who inhale the smoke in the room—"passive smoking." You also set a bad example for your children; children in families where one or both parents smoke are much more likely to adopt the habit than kids from smoke-free environments.

The relationship between fitness walking and smoking is this: *nothing* can do much to improve your overall health if you smoke. You need to find the willpower to quit. There are excellent programs to assist you available through local chapters of the American Heart, Lung and Cancer societies. Why not use the same impetus that encouraged you to start fitness walking to help you stop cigarette smoking.

FITNESS WALKING AND HIGH BLOOD PRESSURE

Despite many scientific studies examining the effect of exercise on blood pressure, it isn't yet clear whether a regular fitness walking program helps lower blood pressure; however, there is enough evidence that regular exercise contributes to it to include a fitness walking prescription as a regular component of blood pressure control.

More often than not, individuals who have high blood pressure may also be overweight and weight loss has been clearly shown to bring blood pressure down. Since walking is such an excellent activity to help in weight loss, it can be a big help in reducing blood pressure in overweight individuals.

The best advice is to have your blood pressure checked at least once a year; if you have high blood pressure you should be under a physician's treatment, and a fitness walking program may well be part of that treatment.

WALKING AND WEIGHT LOSS

This topic is so important that we have devoted an entire chapter to it (see Chapter 5). Fitness walking is an excellent way to help lose weight (specifically, to help lose *fat*), whether you just want to shed a few pounds or if you have a serious weight problem.

Approximately 60 percent of people who start running programs stop within three months; the drop-out rates in walking programs are much lower.

THE MENTAL BENEFITS OF FITNESS WALKING

One of the most important benefits of fitness walking comes from simply taking time off from the strains of everyday life. Many walkers report that their fitness walking programs help them deal with the stresses and strains of jobs, family and friends. As one woman at a walking clinic said, "I wouldn't miss my lunch time walk for the world. It clears my head and puts things in perspective."

A number of studies have shown what active people have learned from experience: after getting some exercise, you feel less anxious and think more clearly. Why this occurs is not completely understood, but there are some clues. Catecholamines—substances like adrenaline that are secreted in response to stress—are metabolized during aerobic exercise. While this was important to cavemen who needed adrenaline to run away from woolly mammoths, it just makes you edgy and irritable. A bout of brisk fitness walking may help the body get rid of a hard day's build-up of catecholamines.

Regular exercise can also increase the blood levels of endorphins—naturally secreted hormones that appear to work in the brain to lessen pain and increase your sense of well being. In one recent study published in the *New England Journal of Medicine,* previously inactive woman who started a regular aerobic exercise program had dramatic increases in their blood endorphin levels.

There are many more things to learn about how exercise brings mental benefits, but there is no denying the universal experience of fitness walkers: their exercise brings contentment, clarity and focus to their thinking.

WALKING AND OSTEOPOROSIS

Unless you've had your head buried in sand for the past two years, you've heard plenty about osteoporosis. It is estimated that over fifteen million Americans, mostly women, suffer from this problem. Osteoporosis—progressive thinning of bone, which often accompanies aging, particularly in women—is frequently the underlying cause of hip fractures and other broken bones

"Fitness walking helps clear my head and puts the world in perspective," says adventure walker Jan Reynolds. *Photo: David Brownell*

in the elderly. Weight-bearing exercise such as fitness walking can help prevent osteoporosis in younger women and retard the process in older women.

But regular weight-bearing exercise is only part of the solution; a proper diet with sufficient calcium is equally important. Chapter 6, "Nutrition for the Woman Fitness Walker," describes osteoporosis, who is at risk and the measures you can take to prevent or treat it. If you think you already have osteoporosis, your walking program should be carried out under your physician's supervision to minimize the risk of injury.

FITNESS WALKING FOR CHILDREN AND ADOLESCENTS

Kids are natural walkers (the trouble starts when you try and get them to sit still). Yet, despite the national interest in fitness, there are disturbing reports that the average fitness level of our children has declined in recent years. This is a tragedy. These bad habits developed in childhood are likely to be carried into adult life; an overweight, sedentary child is likely to become an overweight, sedentary adult with all the associated health risks.

Rather than merely setting a positive example for your children with your own fitness walking program, why not take them along sometimes—if they'll be seen with you. Fitness walking is the ideal family activity, as long as you slow down to accommodate the kids' short strides. These walks can be a wonderful way to do something special together, as well as improve the health and fitness of every family member.

Teenage girls, in particular, may have some special fitness considerations that make walking appealing. A 15-year-old girl may still have some baby fat, or she may be filling out in ways she's not happy about. She's probably extremely self-conscious about her weight, and if she's not particularly athletic, she may be reluctant to participate in sports. Through walking—which doesn't have to *look* like exercise—she can discreetly manage her weight. But don't expect her to walk with her mother . . .

FITNESS WALKING AND TOTAL HEALTH

"Okay," you're saying. "Where do I sign?" But this chapter was intended to convince you that fitness walking will improve your health, not to create the impression that it is a cure-all. Fitness walking must be included in an overall approach to total health. This means paying attention to *all* of the daily practices and habits that have an impact on your health. This includes keeping your cardiac risk factors to a minimum (don't smoke; eat a low-fat, high-fiber, low-cholesterol diet; keep your blood pressure under good control and achieve or maintain optimal weight). It also includes health practices such as regular checkups with a physician and dentist, and self-exam for breast cancer. Even such measures as getting adequate sleep and wearing a seat belt are part of this approach.

For physical conditioning, fitness walking is a great start. However, by combining fitness walking with some low-weight, high-repetition weight work, you'll also build muscular strength and endurance. Proper stretching to improve flexibility is another important feature of an overall program.

All of these considerations may seem a bit far afield in a book on fitness walking, yet, walking works best as a health promoting activity when combined with other good habits and practices. With your fitness walking program as the cornerstone of your overall approach to health and fitness, you're bound to succeed.

Walking is an action that uses almost all of the body's 206 bones and 660 muscles.

2
Getting Started

Doris Reimiller, 55, wanted to lose some weight. Her husband, Dick, 53, wanted to drop a few pounds, too; he also wanted to quit smoking after forty-two years. The Reimillers decided to experiment with a walking program, and found that it helped them both meet their goals. Six months later, Doris—thirty-two pounds lighter—and Dick—smoke-free and down forty-eight pounds—are still walking and loving it.

Lynda had a hard time getting out the door every morning for her walk, even though she loved it once she got going. This puzzled her. She liked exercising and the benefits she reaped, so why the motivation problem? She discussed this with a friend and they decided they needed each other to provide company and a commitment, and one of them always has enough energy to get them both going.

Eileen, a nursing student, came home exhausted from a long day, with much studying still ahead. A friend managed to talk her into going for a little exercise, even though it was the last thing she felt like doing. Upon returning from her walk, she was amazed how energized and awake she felt. Now she considers it a challenge, not a chore, to go out walking. She looks forward to her new-found vitality.

Getting the most out of fitness walking requires some attention to technique, reasonable goals and, by far the toughest part, a personal commitment to "put it all together." Sometimes just the thought of starting a regular activity seems overwhelming. Keep in mind that this is not an unusual response, and you are not alone. Most women feel they have little energy to spare in a day; especially to find time for themselves. But like Eileen, the nursing student, you may find that a little exercise gives you more energy with which to tackle your busy day. If you don't believe this, you'll have a hard time sticking with your program. So, set aside some time in the next day or so and just take a walk. If it makes you feel good, read on about getting more from your walking.

TECHNIQUE

No, you don't need to learn technique. Walking's greatest value as a fitness activity is that you can just go out and do it. But like other sports activities, technique becomes a factor in developing a more effective program. In fitness walking, the de-

velopment of proper technique involves a correct stride, arm swing, head and shoulder position and a steady pace.

Although it's fun to experiment with techniques and learn what your body can do, it is by no means mandatory in walking. You know how to walk, and there's no reason to complicate a refreshingly simple activity. First and foremost, walking should be pleasurable; if you do want to try it with a slightly different twist, here are some tips.

Anne demonstrates three walking strides: a stroll (approximately three miles per hour), with arms swinging loosely at her sides; brisk walking (approximately four miles per hour), with accompanying energetic arm motion; brisk striding (approximately five miles per hour). Here the stride lengthens and arms pump to assist in the vigorous walking motion. *Photo: David Brownell*

STRIDE. • Your stride should be natural and comfortable. Don't make the mistake of taking too long a stride—you'll feel awkward and quickly exhausted. Instead, simply lean forward at your ankles (not at your waist), relax and let your body pick its own stride. This self-selected stride will be most efficient for you.

POSTURE. • If you keep your eyes straight ahead and your chin up while incorporating the forward lean, you'll find that your posture will become almost perfect with no extra effort. Once you've become a regular walker, you may find that you retain this erect and confident posture throughout your day.

ARM SWING. • Walking can be a total body activity—if you don't let your arms dangle like cooked spaghetti at your sides. Still, the arm swing should not be a forced and awkward movement: the natural rhythm of your body will propel the opposite arm forward as your leg strides out. All you have to do is relax your shoulders and let yourself flow.

Your arms can play a more active role if you want to walk more vigorously. Simply continue the same rhythm with your arms bent at the elbow. The angulation can range from a slight bend to 90 degrees. You'll be surprised by the speed you'll gain from this minimal change.

WARM-UP

Your body is like your car—it just won't work right if you don't allow it to warm up first. Many people don't take time to warm up; they begin walking at full speed, which can lead to an injury. A number of recent medical studies have also shown that allowing your heart rate to rise slowly into the target training zone avoids unnecessary cardiac strain.

In addition to loosening up your body for fitness walking, a proper warm-up will help you prepare mentally. Use your warm-up time to focus your thoughts on the exercise that you are about to perform. Think positively about your goals for this walk: more arm action, better posture, etc. This will help you make the shift from your previous activities to your walking frame of mind.

The best warm-up regimen is a slowly progressive period of

walking—to bring your heart rate into the target training zone—followed by a period of gentle stretching to loosen muscles and tendons.

Walk for five to ten minutes, starting out slowly and increasing your pace until you feel your muscles loosening. Then pause to perform the stretching exercises outlined below.

STRETCHING

Rule number one: Always stretch with a slow, steady movement. Bouncing is not only ineffective but can also cause injuries. The goal is to extend and relax your muscles, and when you bounce, your muscles respond by contracting to protect themselves. Thorough stretching takes time—it is best to stretch each muscle for twenty to thirty seconds. Stretching should feel good and relaxing; pain is a warning sign. If you start to feel discomfort while stretching, you've gone far enough. Breathe regularly during stretches. When you are pressed for time there is a temptation to skip the stretching; this is a potentially painful mistake. The benefits in terms of flexibility, improved performance and injury prevention cannot be emphasized enough. It is even helpful to take time during your day while watching television or sitting at a desk to perform some additional stretching to help increase your flexibility.

(Following are some illustrations of Anne performing stretches.)

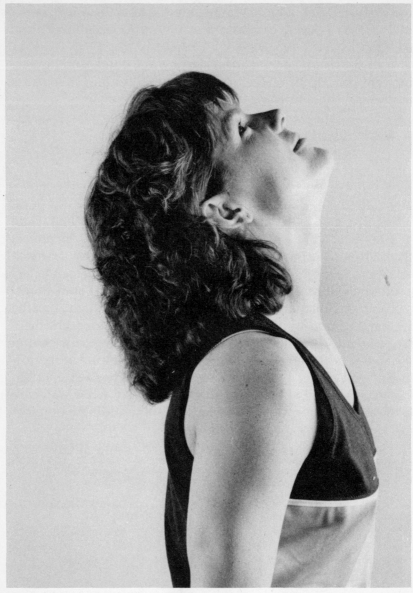

Neck stretch: Slowly lift your chin up as far as you can, tilting your head back, then slowly bring your chin down to touch your chest. Repeat two to three times. *Photo: David Brownell*

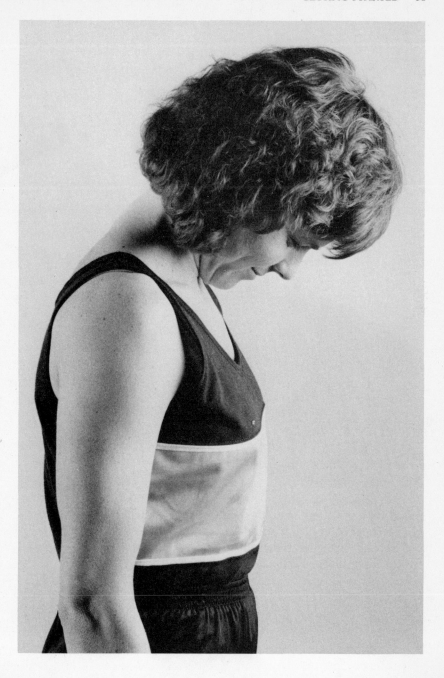

Stand with your feet shoulder-width apart. Slowly try to touch your left ear to your left shoulder without lifting your shoulders up. Repeat with your right ear toward your right shoulder. Repeat two to three times. *Photo: David Brownell*

Neck stretch: Slowly turn your head to the left side and glance over your left shoulder without moving any other body parts. Repeat in the opposite direction. Repeat to each side two to three times. *Photo: David Brownell*

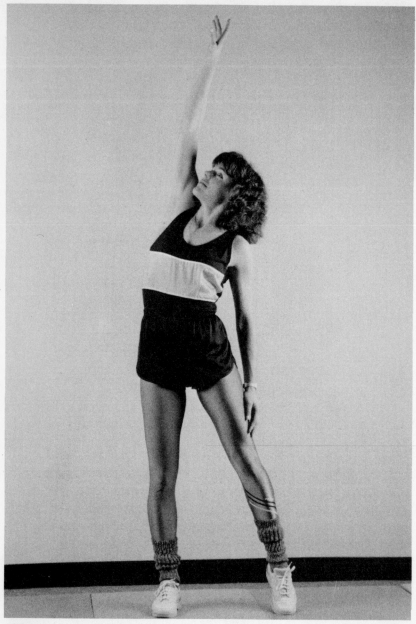

"Reach for the Sky" with your left hand and then your right hand. Stand with feet shoulder-width apart. Repeat to each side four to five times. *Photo: David Brownell*

Shoulder shrugs: Stand with feet shoulder-width apart, lift shoulders to ears and then relax. Repeat four to five times. Shoulder rolls: After the shoulder shrugs, bring your shoulders up, back, down and forward. Repeat four to five times in each direction.
Photo: David Brownell

Triceps stretch: Lift your right arm over your head and place your right hand between your shoulder blades. With your other hand gently push downward on your elbow. Hold for fifteen seconds, then switch arms. Repeat one to two times. *Photo: David Brownell*

Side stretch: Stand with right arm over your head and bend your trunk directly to the left, keeping both of your feet flat. Hold for fifteen seconds, change arms and bend to the other side. Repeat four to five times to each side. *Photo: David Brownell*

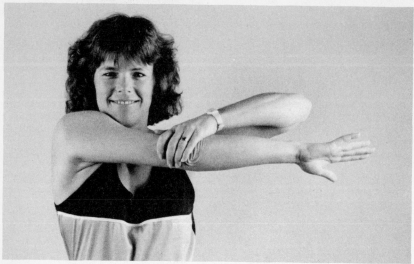

Deltoid stretch: Stand with feet shoulder-width apart. Grasp your right elbow with your left hand and gently pull your right arm across your body. Hold for fifteen seconds, then switch arms. *Photo: David Brownell*

Lower back stretch: Lie on your back with both knees bent, feet flat on the floor. Hug one knee toward you as far as you can. Hold for fifteen to twenty seconds. Repeat with the other leg. *Photo: David Brownell*

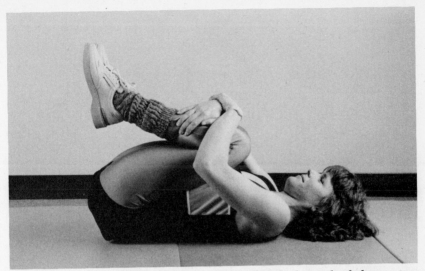

Lower leg stretch: After the lower back stretch, bring both knees to your chest and hold for twenty to thirty seconds. *Photo: David Brownell*

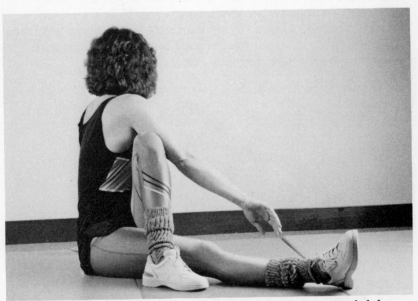

Hip and back stretch: Sit with your back erect. Cross your left leg over your right leg, placing your foot flat. Place your right elbow behind your left knee and gently pull across your body. *Photo: David Brownell*

Groin stretch: Sit with the soles of your feet together and your back straight. Draw your feet toward you as close as you can. Grasp your ankles and press your knees downward. Hold fifteen seconds. Perform two to three times; then slide your feet out about six inches and gently lean out toward your feet, keeping your back straight. Hold for fifteen seconds. *Photo: David Brownell*

Leg stretch: Sit with one leg extended and toes pointed upward. Lean over your extended leg until you feel a slight "pull" in the back of your leg. Hold fifteen seconds. Repeat using each leg two to three times. *Photo: David Brownell*

Back and leg stretch: Sit with both legs extended, toes pointed upward. Lean out between your legs until you feel a slight pull. Hold for fifteen seconds. *Photo: David Brownell*

Side stretch: After the back and leg stretch, clasp your hands behind your head. Try to touch your left elbow to your left knee. Repeat on the right side. Repeat four to five times. *Photo: David Brownell*

Calf stretch: Stand with one leg in front of you and bend the knee. Keep the other leg straight. Lean forward over the bent knee, keeping your lower back straight. Hold for twenty seconds and then repeat with other leg forward. If you have trouble feeling a stretch, try a wider stance. *Photo: David Brownell*

Ankle circles: Stand on your left foot and balance on the ball of your right foot. Slowly rotate the right ankle. Repeat on the opposite side. Repeat on each side four to five times. *Photo: David Brownell*

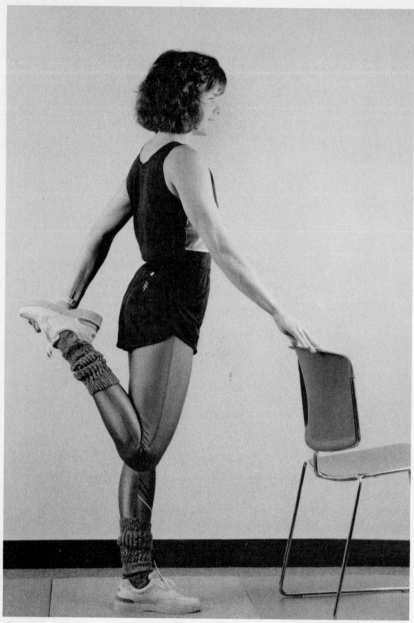

Quadriceps stretch: Using a chair for balance, stand on the left leg and grasp your right foot as shown. Pull the foot upward until a slight tugging sensation is felt on the front of the right thigh. Hold for fifteen seconds. Repeat on the other side. *Photo: David Brownell*

THE AEROBIC TRAINING PHASE

After you've warmed up, you're ready to roll. Your walk should be comfortable and enjoyable, but while you're out there, why not be sure you're getting full cardiovascular benefit? One way to do this is to follow the guidelines in the Rockport Fitness Walking Test (chapters 3 and 4). A less precise, but safe prescription for aerobic training is walking three to five times per week, for thirty to sixty minutes, in your training zone—60 percent to 80 percent of maximum heart rate. Monitoring your heart rate is the best way to know if you're approaching your limits, or if you're ready to challenge yourself further.

To determine your maximum heart rate and training zone, use this formula:

1. Determine your maximum heart rate by subtracting your age in years from 220;
2. Multiply your maximum heart rate by 0.6 and 0.8 to determine your target training zone.

For a 45-year-old walker, the equation works like this:

Maximum heart rate: $220 - 45 \quad = \quad 175$
Target training zone: $175 \times 0.6 \quad = \quad 105$
$175 \times 0.8 \quad = \quad 140$

The target training zone for this fitness walker is 105 to 140 beats per minute.

To take your pulse, gently put your second and third fingers (not your thumb) on your wrist, over the radial artery just inside the wrist bone or over the carotid artery at the neck next to your Adam's apple. Count your pulse for fifteen seconds and multiply by four to determine your resting pulse per minute (between 50 and 90 beats per minute is normal).

Take your pulse for fifteen seconds every five minutes when you begin an exercise program. Start counting your pulse as soon as you stop to get an accurate estimate of your intensity. If you are below your target training zone, you should increase your walking pace; if you are above, decrease it. Eventually you'll be able to estimate your heart rate and walking pace with fewer actual measurements. Also monitor how you feel: if you are breathless while you exercise, or still tired two hours later, you're working too hard and should decrease your intensity or duration.

COOL-DOWN

The cool-down period is as important as the warm-up, and is performed similarly. After the aerobic portion of your walk, cool-down starts with a slow decrease in speed. Using the car analogy, it's like downshifting gears. After four to five minutes of slower walking, stop and stretch again. Trying to save time by skipping the cool-down won't help you in the long run. You'll avoid soreness and enhance flexibility with just a few minutes of stretching, focusing on those areas where you are tightest. Stretching at the end of the workout is more effective because your muscles and tendons are already warm and loose, and can be stretched further.

STAYING WITH IT

Now comes the crucial test of your walking program: sticking with it. Studies have found higher rates of adherence to fitness walking than to other exercise programs, but drop-out rates still range from 25 percent to 50 percent. How can you avoid becoming a statistic? Here are a number of pointers to help you over the obstacles to adherence that many walkers encounter. *SET GOALS AND REWARD YOURSELF.* • Establish a minimum distance you'll walk: two miles, thirty minutes, eighteen telephone poles. When you reach your goal, give yourself a pat on the back. Decide that you won't call your friend or read your book until after you've walked. Or walk to where you'll meet a friend. Try to maintain a positive attitude—don't wake up asking yourself *if* you will walk today, but rather *when* you

---

Walking along a rough but relatively level trail requires 50 percent more energy expenditure than walking on a paved road.

will walk today. These goals may seem elementary, but they can make the difference until you get hooked, and walking becomes its own reward.

WALK WITH A FRIEND. • Remember the example of Lynda and her friend? A walking partner not only makes the activity social and more fun, it gives you a commitment to another person—a strong motivator.

BATTLE BOREDOM. • One of the greatest enemies of exercise is boredom—the monotony of the same old routine. The answer to that problem is simply variety: find new routes, other partners, a music headset (although they are not advisable near traffic); walk at different speeds; walk backward. Anything that will break the tedium can keep you going. Be alert to the possibility of "burn out" and *before* it strikes, change your routine.

JOIN A CLUB. • Athletic clubs in many cities are forming walking clubs and giving classes to teach the benefits of the sport as well as techniques to improve performance. Some of these classes move indoors during the winter months and incorporate circuit training with weights.

TRAIN FOR AN EVENT. • Organized striding events in which thousands of people walk courses—usually six miles—are becoming increasingly popular. These noncompetitive events attract participants of all ages and fitness levels; they're healthy and fun—almost paradelike.

RECORD YOUR PROGRESS. • Once you have started a walking program, you may want to keep track of such things as mileage, exercise heart rate, time, weather conditions and feelings about yourself. Marking down progress is motivational, and it's also rewarding to watch your distance or speed go up while your weight, resting heart rate, waistline, etc., go down.

EQUIPMENT

As more people turn their attention to fitness walking, more equipment becomes available to make the sport safer, more comfortable, and more enjoyable. While necessary gear is minimal, proper clothing and footwear can make an enormous difference to a fitness walker.

The most important piece of equipment for the serious walker is a properly designed pair of walking shoes. Over the past several years, considerable advances have been made in the design of walking shoes. Much of the information needed to make these changes has come from scientific investigations in the area of biomechanics. In this field, the motions of any particular activity are broken down into very small segments using high-speed filming techniques and computer technology. In addition, the forces involved are measured by use of a force plate.

When biomechanics has been applied to fitness walking, it has been discovered that the walking stride is unique and very different from the running stride. In the running motion, the individual typically lands with significant weight on the heel, then rapidly transfers this weight to the ball of the foot as he or she springs off the ground. In walking, the heel hits at a greater angle than in running, and the weight is slowly rolled forward on to the ball of the foot.

The forces involved in the walking stride are also significantly less than those in the running stride. In running, you land with three to four times your body weight every time your foot hits the ground, whereas in walking, since one foot is always in contact with the ground, the forces are 1 to 1.25 times your body weight on each stride.

Over the past three years, our laboratory, in conjunction with the Biomechanics Laboratory at the University of Massachusetts/Amherst, has been involved in a number of studies of the biomechanics of walking. We have made a number of important findings. First, we discovered that a properly designed walking shoe is better able to cushion the impact on the heel during fitness walking than a comparably priced athletic shoe. Second, we found that well-designed walking shoes were better able to control excessive pronation (the tendency of the heel to rotate from outside to inside) during fitness walking than comparably priced athletic shoes. Finally, we found that women land with more pressure on their heels than men do during fitness walking when the forces are normalized for weight.

What is the significance of this information for the average fitness walker? First, our research clearly supports the concept that a properly designed shoe is best for safe and enjoyable fitness walking. Second, this research also suggests that the

It takes 60 to 70 percent more energy to walk in high heels than flat-soled shoes.

biomechanical characteristics of fitness walking for women may be slightly different from those for men. Thus, a woman should look for a particularly well-designed walking shoe and ideally one made specifically for women.

Several years ago, many people doubted that there was a need for shoes specifically designed for walking. However, research in our laboratory and at other laboratories makes it clear that each activity has its own unique biomechanical needs and hence deserves its own piece of specifically designed equipment. This is completely consistent with the history of other activities where advanced technology has led to improved performance, safety and pleasure.

Anne discusses the construction of a properly designed shoe for fitness walking. The "heel counter" is particularly important since women land with more force on their heels per body weight than men at any given walking speed. *Photo: David Brownell*

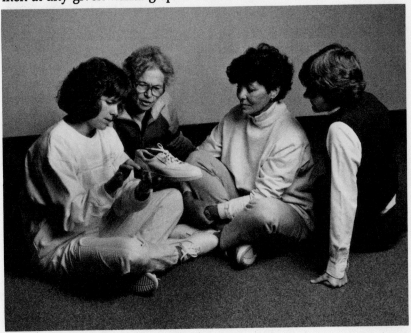

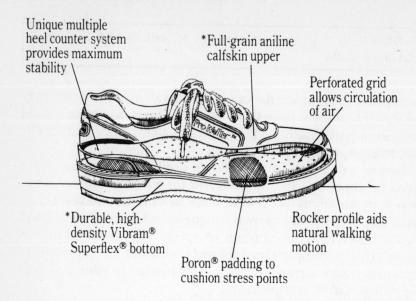

Unique multiple
heel counter system
provides maximum
stability

*Full-grain aniline
calfskin upper

Perforated grid
allows circulation
of air

*Durable, high-
density Vibram®
Superflex® bottom

Poron® padding to
cushion stress points

Rocker profile aids
natural walking
motion

Take the modern ski boot for example. It is a far cry from the old leather lace-up models and has made skiing safer and more fun. Or take the tennis racket, golf club, or football helmet. In virtually every form of human endeavor, advanced technology has led to enhanced safety, performance and enjoyment. Fitness walking is no different from these other activities. People who doubt the need for a specialized walking shoe are simply forgetting the historic relationship between activity, sport and technology. As fitness walkers make more demands on the activity, technology will respond with lighter weight, more comfortable, more durable, safer walking shoes. There are already some excellent biomechanically engineered walking shoes available.

What should the serious fitness walker look for in a walking shoe? A number of features are important. When you choose a shoe for fitness walking you should look for one that gives you support and comfort. There is general agreement that a number of features should be included in a well designed shoe for fitness walking. Some of the features are shown on the diagram above and described here.

HEEL CUSHIONING. · The heel takes the largest forces on impact during fitness walking. Therefore, it is particularly important to have a well-cushioned heel. This is especially important for women.

LIGHT WEIGHT. • A considerable amount of extra work can be done by wearing shoes that are too heavy. A well-designed walking shoe should be lightweight.

FIRM HEEL COUNTER. • When the foot hits the ground during fitness walking there is a tendency for it to pronate. Pronation is part of the body's mechanism for "braking" so it is not desirable to eliminate it entirely. It is important, however, to control *excessive* pronation since this can expose the foot, ankle, knee and hip to strain and potential injury. Therefore, a fitness walker should look for a shoe that has a good mechanism for "cupping" the heel. This is typically done with an internal and/or external heel counter.

INTERNAL CUSHIONING AND SUPPORT SYSTEM. • The innersole mechanism in a fitness walking shoe should help cushion the foot during walking. Most modern walking shoes utilize some type of formed "orthotic," which is fitted inside the shoe.

OUTERSOLE. • The outersole should be reasonably soft—you should be able to indent it with your fingernail. It should also be made of a durable material that has some "bounce" in it. The shape of the outersole should also accommodate the unique biomechanical needs of fitness walking. Several types of shoes now incorporate a "rocker" profile to aid in the natural biomechanical motion that occurs when the weight is slowly transferred from the heel to the toe during fitness walking. The sole of a walking shoe should be less flexible than that of a running shoe since it is more important for the walking shoe to provide support during the relatively slow transfer of weight during fitness walking than it is to flex and allow the rapid transfer of weight that occurs in running. Excessive flexibility in the sole of the shoe will lead to foot muscle fatigue.

UPPER CONSTRUCTION. • The optimum materials for a walking shoe are leather or a combination of leather and fabric. This allows breathability and support in the shoe. These materials allow excellent support, which is so essential to minimize foot and leg muscle fatigue, particularly during long walks.

TOE BOX. • A roomy toe box is important to allow the toes to spread out during the "push off" phase of fitness walking.

Proper shoe care is important. You should allow your shoes to dry out completely after a vigorous fitness walk. Remember, socks are important not only to protect your feet but also prevent excessive moisture from damaging your shoes.

People often ask us how they should select a shoe for fitness walking. First, you should pay attention to all of the information outlined above. Second, try on the shoes in the shoe store and try to walk around the shoe store at a pace that will be consistent with the kind of pace you will use during your fitness walk. Finally, all shoe clerks should know that it is no longer acceptable to say that "any good shoe will serve for walking." There are very well designed shoes on the market made specifically for fitness walking, and we strongly encourage you to purchase this one essential piece of equipment. This will enhance your pleasure and enjoyment during fitness walking.

WEATHER

While rain or extreme temperatures may seem daunting at first, walking in these conditions is not only possible, but often particularly enjoyable. The trick is to dress properly and protect yourself from the elements.

WET WEATHER. • There are many excellent water-resistant materials on the market—Gore-Tex, Versa Tec, etc. While this gear may seem expensive initially, it can turn a rainy day from a wash-out into a delight. Rob Sweetgall, who walked 11,208 miles across America a few years ago, cannot say enough about the all-weather gear that kept him happy and dry from coast to coast.

WARM WEATHER. • The dangers of walking—or doing any strenuous exercise—in hot weather should not be underestimated. Heat stress and heat stroke strike large numbers of exercisers in hot climates. Heat stress is a function of air temperature, humidity, direct sunlight, wind and level of physical activity. All of these factors increase the heat load, except wind,

On the average a woman produces about one and one-half pints of sweat a day in temperate conditions.

Sunburn can occur on long walks. Always wear a hat to protect the skin and hair when out for long walks, particularly in the middle of the day.

which promotes cooling through evaporation of sweat. Heat stress can be avoided by wearing light, loose-fitting clothing, drinking six to eight ounces of water every twenty to thirty minutes, walking in the early morning and evening and decreasing your pace. Wearing rubberized suits, sweat shirts or sweat pants in hot weather will not help you lose weight any faster by making you sweat more. Instead this type of clothing can cause dangerously high body temperatures.

Symptoms of heat stress include dizziness, headache, abdominal cramps and an absence of perspiration. At the first sign of heat stress, get out of the heat immediately, rest, and drink as much water as you can. A chart has been developed below that uses temperature and relative humidity (available from weather forecasts) to set guidelines for exercise. Cardiac patients and older individuals especially should follow the guidelines carefully.

The Temperature and Humidity Guide indicates at which temperature and humidity conditions it is safe to walk.

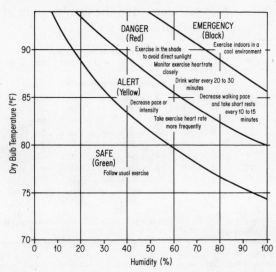

> **Seventy percent of the body heat dissipated during exercise is lost through your head and hands.**

COOL WEATHER. · A walk in the cold can be refreshing and invigorating—especially once you're back inside with a cup of coffee or hot chocolate. Air as cold as −20 degrees Fahrenheit (F) generally does not damage the respiratory passages. But hypothermia—the loss of warmth from the core of the body— is life-threatening, and should be watched for carefully whenever the temperature is below 50 degrees F. Wind speeds up heat loss; this is what is meant by the wind chill factor. For example, a 40 degrees F reading is equivalent to 18 degrees F when the wind speed is 20 mph. In addition, walking against the wind increases the cooling effect of the wind in direct relation to walking pace. Use the wind chill chart and the following guidelines to avoid problems during cold weather.

1. Cover all parts of the body to prevent heat loss, especially your head and hands.
2. Wear layers of clothing that can be unzipped and removed as you get warmer. Loose clothing that traps layers of dead air space provides good insulation.

The Wind Chill Index indicates when the combination of cold weather and wind makes it unsafe to walk.

				Actual Thermometer Reading (F)							
	50	40	30	20	10	0	−10	−20	−30	−40	−50	−60
Wind Speed in MPH					Equivalent Temperature (F)							
Calm	50	40	30	20	10	0	−10	−20	−30	−40	−50	−60
5	48	37	27	16	6	−5	−15	−26	−36	−47	−57	−68
10	40	28	16	4	−9	−21	−33	−46	−58	−70	−83	−95
15	36	22	9	−5	−18	−36	−45	−58	−72	−85	−99	−112
20	32	18	4	−10	−25	−39	−53	−67	−82	−96	−110	−124
25	30	16	0	−15	−29	−44	−59	−74	−88	−104	−118	−133
30	28	13	−2	−18	−33	−48	−63	−79	−94	−109	−125	−140
35	27	11	−4	−20	−35	−49	−67	−82	−98	−113	−129	−145
40	26	10	−6	−21	−37	−53	−69	−85	−100	−116	−132	−148

(Wind speeds greater than 40 MPH have little additional effect	LITTLE DANGER (for properly clothed person)	INCREASING DANGER	GREAT DANGER
		Danger from freezing of exposed flesh	

3. Nylon wind suits can help decrease the effect of wind.
4. Water—both rain and sweat—drastically increases the rate of heat loss. Wear rainproof gear, and remove damp or wet clothing as soon as you stop exercising. Remember that if you're wet, hypothermia can strike at temperatures well above freezing.
5. If it's windy, try starting out against the wind and return with it at your back.

TRAFFIC

Cars (and bikes) are the walker's biggest enemies, next to dogs. If you walk in the city, you know this, and you know that it's up to you to look out for them. Traffic is always a concern in bad weather as vision is impaired and drivers are not prepared to look for walkers. Always walk facing traffic and watch out for the other guy. Try to walk in daylight, but if you can't, reflective tape located strategically on your shoes and clothes should help avoid dangerous situations.

SURFACES

Footing is another obstacle for walkers and runners. If you run into slick surfaces, try to keep your knees slightly bent and shorten your stride. This will give you more stability if you slip.

When walking uphill, walk slowly and lean forward to get more power. Going downhill, take short, low steps to minimize the shock of landing.

FOOT CARE

"My feet are my Cadillacs," says ultra-walker Sweetgall. These tips on proper foot care can save you from a number of the painful pitfalls of pounding the pavement:

Walking for half an hour in heavy New York City traffic is the equivalent of smoking one-half to one pack of cigarettes.

1. Make sure that your shoes fit properly—nothing causes blisters more quickly than ill-fitting shoes;
2. Wear light, comfortable socks made of either cotton or a cotton/Orlon fiber blend, which "wick" moisture away from your skin;
3. Pay attention to "hot spots" on your feet; a burning sensation on a patch of skin on your foot is often the first stage of a blister;
4. Keep your feet clean and dry; make sure to towel your feet before and after your fitness walk;
5. Keep your toenails trimmed short, and always cut them straight across—not rounded;
6. If you have problems with corns or callouses, see a podiatrist; trying to self-treat these conditions is an invitation to infection;
7. It's estimated that three out of four people experience low-threshold pain in their feet every day, but there's no reason to suffer; if you have any questions about specific conditions, or you develop a painful foot problem, see a doctor . . . often, custom orthotics or inserts available in drug and sporting goods stores can make all the difference.

3
Testing Yourself for Fitness Walking

Nothing kills good intentions like unrealistic expectations. Many women simply expect too much from themselves, too fast. They end up getting frustrated, or burned out, or worse, injured. A good way to avoid this is to test your aerobic capacity to determine what you're ready for, and then select a program that's appropriate for your level of fitness.

Testing can help you maintain enthusiasm, too. Periodic testing will show improvement of conditioning as you continue to exercise, and help you set new goals, if you so desire.

Over the past two years, extensive testing has been done at the Exercise Physiology Laboratory at the University of Massachusetts Medical School to develop a fitness test based entirely on walking. What has resulted is the first scientifically validated test of cardiovascular fitness based entirely on walking. The test is called the Rockport Fitness Walking Test. Before getting to the test itself, it's important to address a few issues about cardiac and physical fitness testing.

WHO NEEDS TO SEE A PHYSICIAN?

If you're over the age of 45 and wish to start a fitness walking program (or *any* exercise program), you should obtain a physician's clearance. The same is true, regardless of age, if you have been inactive or are overweight, or if you have any history of heart trouble, risk factors for heart disease (such as cigarette smoking, high blood pressure or high cholesterol) or any orthopedic problems.

If you already have a good relationship with your physician, this may just mean a phone call. More likely, your doctor will want you to come for an evaluation.

This kind of checkup is never a bad idea, and a visit to your physician can provide assurance that starting an exercise program is safe for you. The examination should include measurement of your blood pressure and heart rate, as well as listening to your heart with a stethoscope. A resting electrocardiogram may also be taken, and in some instances your physician may recommend an exercise tolerance test on the treadmill. An exercise tolerance test is the best screening procedure to determine if you have underlying disease of the coronary arteries, which causes angina and heart attacks.

If you are given an exercise tolerance test, you will be asked to walk and/or run at progressively higher speeds on a treadmill while your heart is carefully monitored. The physician looks to see if any dangerous changes occur in the electrical pattern of your heart as it speeds up during exercise.

THE ROCKPORT FITNESS WALKING TEST

Despite the fact that an estimated fifty-five million Americans list walking as their favorite form of exercise, up until recently no laboratory had ever developed a scientifically validated test of cardiovascular fitness based on walking. Most fitness tests consisted of running, stationary cycling, or bench-stepping exercises, which are either unfamiliar to or extremely demanding for many people. A test was needed that could be safely and easily given to individuals of all ages and all fitness levels.

In 1984, the Exercise Physiology Laboratory at the University of Massachusetts Medical School and Department of Exercise Science at U/Mass Amherst undertook the development of a scientifically valid test based on walking. The project took almost two years to complete. It was the most exhaustive inquiry into walking ever performed.

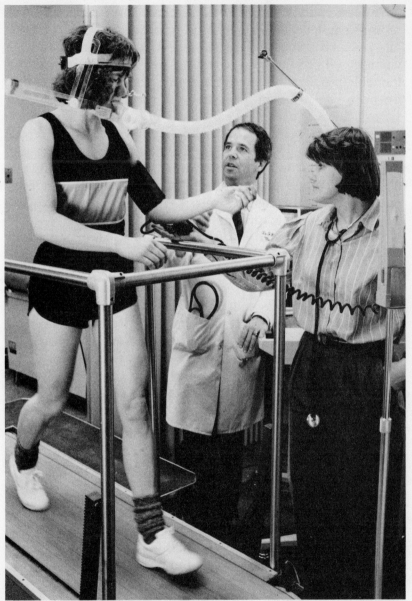

Dr. Rippe and Dr. Ward test Anne Kashiwa at the University of Massachusetts Medical School Exercise Physiology Laboratory on sophisticated equipment used to analyze her oxygen consumption. This type of test was performed on 343 individuals to establish the scientific validity of the Rockport Fitness Walking Test. *Photo: David Brownell*

The test you will actually take at home is very *simple*, yet the process employed to establish its validity was quite complex. The research subjects were 343 individuals (165 men and 178 women), all of whom were free of any known cardiac or orthopedic problems. None were on medication known to affect the heart rate or blood pressure response to exercise.

Test subjects over 40 years old were first examined by a cardiologist. All subjects then underwent a maximum exercise tolerance test on a treadmill. During this test, direct measurements were taken of each subject's expired air to determine the maximum oxygen consumption (VO_2 max). The VO_2 max is regarded by physicians and exercise physiologists as the "gold standard" of aerobic capacity.

The equipment used to directly measure VO_2 max involves attaching the research subject to a mouthpiece, which in turn is attached to a complicated piece of equipment that allows analysis of the expired gases. This "metabolic cart," controlled by a computer, was initially developed for the space program.

Following the treadmill test, on at least two separate days subjects were taken to a nearby outdoor quarter-mile track. At the track they were asked to walk a mile as briskly as possible, maintaining a steady pace. While they were walking, their heart rates were continuously monitored using telemetry equipment. Their time to walk the mile was also carefully measured by the research team. Subjects had to walk a mile on at least two separate days or until the times they achieved for the two miles were within thirty seconds of each other.

Once all the research subjects had undergone the treadmill test and at least two track walks, all the experimental data were entered into the mainframe computer at U/Mass Amherst.

What emerged was a safe, easy, highly accurate test of cardiovascular capacity. It's just as valid for a 25-year-old woman as it is for a 65-year-old woman, and it's at least as accurate as any other cardiovascular fitness test ever developed for use outside the laboratory. But most important, it's designed specifically for walkers.

Test Yourself

The only preparation you'll need is to familiarize yourself with taking your pulse, and find a flat, measured mile to walk. Instructions on taking your pulse are in Chapter 2. Most high schools and recreation facilities have a track—most, but not all, are a quarter mile. Make sure you know the exact measurement. If you measure out your own mile, do it on a flat road with no interruptions (e.g., stop lights).

The test involves three simple steps. First, walk the mile as fast as you can. Walk comfortably, but briskly—you should be able to maintain a steady pace. Second, record your time to the nearest second. Most people walk between 3.0 and 6.0 miles per hour, so it would take between ten and twenty minutes to walk the mile. Third, record your heart rate immediately at the end of the mile. Measure it as soon as you stop, since it begins to slow almost immediately.

Record Your Results

AGE: _____ YEARS
TIME TO WALK A MILE: _____ MINUTES, _____ SECONDS
HEART RATE AT THE END OF THE MILE: _____ BEATS/MINUTE

To determine your fitness level turn to the appropriate Relative Fitness Level chart for your age and sex. This shows the relative fitness level of others of your age adapted from established fitness norms set by the American Heart Association. If you are under 20, you can safely use the charts for 20–29-year-olds; similarly, if you are over 80, the chart for ages 60 plus is appropriate for you, as well. If you are over 90 and still walking, you don't need this test—whatever you've been doing up to this point has been right!

Now, mark the point on the chart defined by your walking time and heart rate at the end of the walk to compare your performance with that of others in your age category.

Let us give you an example of how this is done. Joan is a 45-year-old walker. Her results are as follows:

AGE: *45* years
TIME TO WALK A MILE: *15* minutes, *30* seconds
HEART RATE AT THE END OF THE MILE: *130* beats/minute

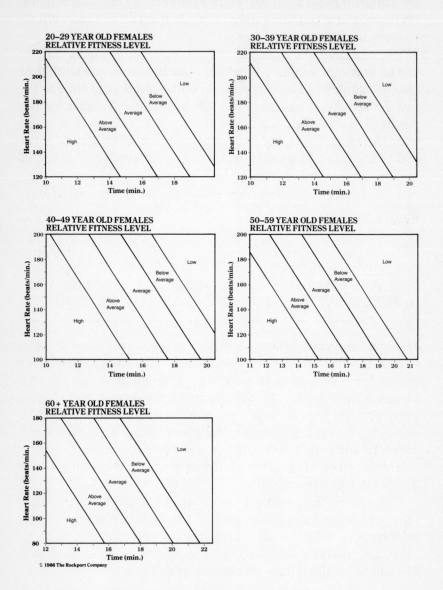

© 1986 The Rockport Walking Institute

To determine her cardiovascular fitness level compared with other women her age, Joan turns to the chart marked 40–49-YEAR-OLD FEMALES and draws in lines representing her time and heart rate. This chart was developed assuming a 125 pound female. Her results are illustrated at left. As you can see, Joan's results put her in the "above average" category.

In the next chapter, you'll use your test results to select the twenty-week walking prescription geared to your level of fitness.

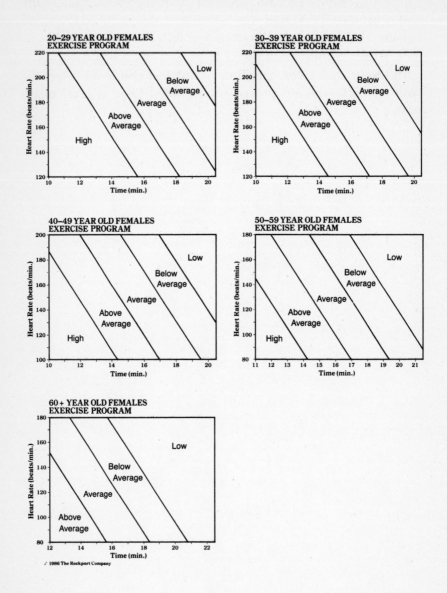

20–29 YEAR OLD FEMALES EXERCISE PROGRAM

30–39 YEAR OLD FEMALES EXERCISE PROGRAM

40–49 YEAR OLD FEMALES EXERCISE PROGRAM

50–59 YEAR OLD FEMALES EXERCISE PROGRAM

60+ YEAR OLD FEMALES EXERCISE PROGRAM

© 1986 The Rockport Company

© 1986 The Rockport Walking Institute

4

Fitness Walking Programs for Women

Now that you know your relative fitness level, you're ready to choose the walking program that will be right for you—vigorous enough to work your body, but not overly taxing. These programs were designed to correspond to the fitness levels in the test, from the most strenuous program for a high aerobic capacity, to the least demanding program for a low level. Simply plot your one-mile walk time and finishing heart rate on the chart for women your age, then turn to the appropriate twenty-week program.

Let's use Joan as an example again. Recall that her results from the Rockport Fitness Walking Test were:

Age: 45 years
Time to walk the mile: 15 minutes, 30 seconds
Heart rate at the end of the mile: 130 beats/minute

Turning to the Exercise Program chart for 40–49-year-olds and plotting her time and heart rate gives the result illustrated at left.

Joan's result places her in the average area, so she would follow the twenty-week average exercise program.

HOW OFTEN TO TEST YOURSELF

The most important benefits from fitness walking come when you adopt programs that are consistent and lifelong. Frequent retesting tends to focus your attention on short-term goals, so try to wait the entire twenty weeks before you test yourself again. If you want to perform a preliminary test, wait until you have completed at least ten weeks of your walking program. This way, you're more likely to see some heartening results.

To retest yourself, simply repeat the test and plot your new time and heart rate on the appropriate charts. If you find you are ready to move to the next exercise program, you can start that program in the middle—around week ten. This is because your old program has taken you beyond the beginning stages of the next level.

By the time you reach the average, above average or high level categories you may want to go into a maintenance program. These programs, designed to become lifelong, good fitness habits, are listed in Table 4-6.

The paces listed are only approximations. Speed should be determined by the pace that keeps your heart rate at the appropriate percentage of maximum listed. To learn how to determine your maximum heart rate, see Chapter 2.

TABLE 4-1: LOW LEVEL FITNESS PROGRAM

Week	Warm-up	Mileage	Pace (mph)	Heart Rate (% of max.)	Cool-down	Frequency (times per week)
1	5–7 mins. before-walk stretches	1.0	3.0	60	5–7 mins. after-walk stretches	5
2	5–7 mins.	1.0	3.0	60	5–7 mins.	5
3	5–7 mins.	1.25	3.0	60	5–7 mins.	5
4	5–7 mins.	1.25	3.0	60	5–7 mins.	5
5	5–7 mins.	1.5	3.0	60	5–7 mins.	5
6	5–7 mins.	1.5	3.5	60–70	5–7 mins.	5
7	5–7 mins.	1.75	3.5	60–70	5–7 mins.	5
8	5–7 mins.	1.75	3.5	60–70	5–7 mins.	5
9	5–7 mins.	2.0	3.5	60–70	5–7 mins.	5
10	5–7 mins.	2.0	3.75	60–70	5–7 mins.	5
11	5–7 mins.	2.0	3.75	70	5–7 mins.	5
12	5–7 mins.	2.25	3.75	70	5–7 mins.	5
13	5–7 mins.	2.25	3.75	70	5–7 mins.	5
14	5–7 mins.	2.5	3.75	70	5–7 mins.	5
15	5–7 mins.	2.5	4.0	70	5–7 mins.	5
16	5–7 mins.	2.5	4.0	70	5–7 mins.	5
17	5–7 mins.	2.75	4.0	70–80	5–7 mins.	5
18	5–7 mins.	2.75	4.0	70–80	5–7 mins.	5
19	5–7 mins.	3.0	4.0	70–80	5–7 mins.	5
20	5–7 mins.	3.0	4.0	70–80	5–7 mins.	5

At the end of the twenty-week fitness walking protocol, retest yourself to establish your new program.

TABLE 4-2: BELOW AVERAGE FITNESS LEVEL PROGRAM

Week	Warm-up	Mileage	Pace (mph)	Heart Rate (% of max.)	Cool-down	Frequency (times per week)
1	5–7 mins. before-walk stretches	1.5	3.0	60–70	5–7 mins. after-walk stretches	5
2	5–7 mins.	1.5	3.0	60–70	5–7 mins.	5
3	5–7 mins.	1.75	3.0	60–70	5–7 mns.	5
4	5–7 mins.	1.75	3.0	60–70	5–7 mins.	5
5	5–7 mins.	2.0	3.0	60–70	5–7 mins.	5
6	5–7 mins.	2.0	3.0	60–70	5–7 mins.	5
7	5–7 mins.	2.0	3.5	70	5–7 mins.	5
8	5–7 mins.	2.25	3.5	70	5–7 mins.	5
9	5–7 mins.	2.25	3.5	70	5–7 mins.	5
10	5–7 mins.	2.5	3.5	70	5–7 mins.	5
11	5–7 mins.	2.5	3.5	70	5–7 mins.	5
12	5–7 mins.	2.5	3.5	70	5–7 mins.	5
13	5–7 mins.	2.75	3.5	70	5–7 mins.	5
14	5–7 mins.	2.75	4.0	70–80	5–7 mins.	5
15	5–7 mins.	3.0	4.0	70–80	5–7 mins.	5
16	5–7 mins.	3.0	4.0	70–80	5–7 mins.	5
17	5–7 mins.	3.25	4.0	70–80	5–7 mins.	5
18	5–7 mins.	3.25	4.0	70–80	5–7 mins.	5
19	5–7 mins.	3.5	4.0	70–80	5–7 mins.	5
20	5–7 mins.	3.5	4.0	70–80	5–7 mins	5

At the end of the twenty-week fitness walking protocol, retest yourself to establish your new program.

TABLE 4-3: AVERAGE LEVEL FITNESS PROGRAM

Week	Warm-up	Mileage	Pace (mph)	Heart Rate (% of max.)	Cool-down	Frequency (times per week)
1	5–7 mins. before-walk stretches	2.0	3.0	70	5–7 mins. after-walk stretches	5
2	5–7 mins.	2.25	3.0	70	5–7 mins.	5
3	5–7 mins.	2.5	3.0	70	5–7 mins.	5
4	5–7 mins.	2.5	3.0	70	5–7 mins.	5
5	5–7 mins.	2.75	3.0	70	5–7 mins.	5
6	5–7 mins.	2.75	3.5	70	5–7 mins.	5
7	5–7 mins.	2.75	3.5	70	5–7 mins.	5
8	5–7 mins.	2.75	3.5	70	5–7 mins.	5
9	5–7 mins.	3.0	3.5	70	5–7 mins.	5
10	5–7 mins.	3.0	3.5	70	5–7 mins.	5
11	5–7 mins.	3.0	4.0	70–80	5–7 mins.	5
12	5–7 mins.	3.0	4.0	70–80	5–7 mins	5
13	5–7 mins.	3.25	4.0	70–80	5–7 mins.	5
14	5–7 mins.	3.25	4.0	70–80	5–7 mins.	5
15	5–7 mins.	3.5	4.0	70–80	5–7 mins.	5
16	5–7 mins.	3.5	4.5	70–80	5–7 mins.	5
17	5–7 mins.	3.5	4.5	70–80	5–7 mins.	5
18	5–7 mins.	4.0	4.5	70–80	5–7 mins.	5
19	5–7 mins.	4.0	4.5	70–80	5–7 mins.	5
20	5–7 mins.	4.0	4.5	70–80	5–7 mins.	5

At the end of the twenty-week fitness walking protocol you may either retest yourself and move to a new fitness walking category or turn directly to the Average Level Fitness Maintenance Program for a lifetime of fitness walking.

TABLE 4-4: ABOVE AVERAGE FITNESS LEVEL PROGRAM

Week	Warm-up	Mileage	Pace (mph)	Heart Rate (% of max.)	Cool-down	Frequency (times per week)
1	5–7 mins. before-walk stretches	2.5	3.5	70	5–7 mins. after-walk stretches	5
2	5–7 mins.	2.75	3.5	70	5–7 mins.	5
3	5–7 mins.	3.0	3.5	70	5–7 mins.	5
4	5–7 mins.	3.0	3.5	70	5–7 mins.	5
5	5–7 mins.	3.25	3.5	70	5–7 mins.	5
6	5–7 mins.	3.25	4.0	70–80	5–7 mins.	5
7	5–7 mins.	3.5	4.0	70–80	5–7 mins.	5
8	5–7 mins.	3.75	4.0	70–80	5–7 mins.	5
9	5–7 mins.	4.0	4.0	70–80	5–7 mins.	5
10	5–7 mins.	4.0	4.0	70–80	5–7 mins.	5
11	5–7 mins.	4.0	4.5	70–80	5–7 mins.	5
12	5–7 mins.	4.0	4.5	70–80	5–7 mins.	5
13	5–7 mins.	4.0	4.5	70–80	5–7 mins.	5
14	5–7 mins.	4.0	4.5	70–80	5–7 mins.	5
15	5–7 mins.	4.0	4.5	70–80	5–7 mins.	5
16	5–7 mins.	4.0	4.5	70–80	5–7 mins.	5
17	5–7 mins.	4.0	4.5	70–80	5–7 mins.	5
18	5–7 mins.	4.0	4.5	70–80	5–7 mins.	5
19	5–7 mins.	4.0	4.5	70–80	5–7 mins.	5
20	5–7 mins.	4.0	4.5	70–80	5–7 mins.	5

At the end of the twenty-week fitness walking protocol turn to the Above Average/High Level Fitness Maintenance Program for a lifetime of fitness walking.

TABLE 4-5: HIGH LEVEL FITNESS PROGRAM

Week	Warm-up	Mileage	Pace (mph)	Incline or Weight	Heart Rate (% of max.)	Cool-down	Frequency (times per week)
1	5–7 mins. before-walk stretches	3.0	4.0		70	5–7 mins. after-walk stretches	5
2	5–7 mins.	3.25	4.0	No	70	5–7 mins.	5
3	5–7 mins.	3.5	4.0	No	70	5–7 mins.	5
4	5–7 mins.	3.5	4.5	No	70–80	5–7 mins.	5
5	5–7 mins.	3.75	4.5	No	70–80	5–7 mins.	5
6	5–7 mins.	4.0	4.5	No	70–80	5–7 mins.	5
7	5–7 mins.	4.0	4.5	+	70–80	5–7 mins.	5
8	5–7 mins.	4.0	4.5	+	70–80	5–7 mins.	5
9	5–7 mins.	4.0	4.5	+	70–80	5–7 mins.	5
10	5–7 mins.	4.0	4.5	+	70–80	5–7 mins.	5
11	5–7 mins.	4.0	4.5	+	70–80	5–7 mins.	5
12	5–7 mins.	4.0	4.5	+	70–80	5–7 mins.	5
13	5–7 mins.	4.0	4.5	+	70–80	5–7 mins.	5
14	5–7 mins.	4.0	4.5	+	70–80	5–7 mins.	5
15	5–7 mins.	4.0	4.5	+	70–80	5–7 mins.	5
16	5–7 mins.	4.0	4.5	+	70–80	5–7 mins.	5
17	5–7 mins.	4.0	4.5	+	70–80	5–7 mins.	5
18	5–7 mins.	4.0	4.5	+	70–80	5–7 mins.	5
19	5–7 mins.	4.0	4.5	+	70–80	5–7 mins.	5
20	5–7 mins.	4.0	4.5	+	70–80	5–7 mins.	5

At the end of the twenty-week fitness walking protocol turn to the Above Average/High Level Fitness Maintenance Program for a lifetime of fitness walking.

TABLE 4-6: LIFELONG MAINTENANCE PROGRAMS
AVERAGE LEVEL FITNESS MAINTENANCE PROGRAM

TOTAL TIME: 1 hour
WARM-UP: 5 to 7 minutes of before-walk stretches
AEROBIC WORKOUT: mileage: 4.0
pace: 4.5 miles per hour
HEART RATE: 70 to 80 percent of maximum
COOL-DOWN: 5 to 7 minutes of after-walk stretches
FREQUENCY: 3 to 5 times per week
WEEKLY MILEAGE: 12 to 20 miles

ABOVE AVERAGE/HIGH LEVEL FITNESS
MAINTENANCE PROGRAM

TOTAL TIME: 1 hour
WARM-UP: 5 to 7 minutes of before-walk stretches
AEROBIC WORKOUT: mileage: 4.0
pace: 4.5 miles per hour
weight/incline: weights (to upper body) or
incline
(hill walking may be added as needed to keep
heart rate in target zone—70 to 80 percent of
the predicted maximum)
HEART RATE: 70 to 80 percent of maximum
COOL-DOWN: 5 to 7 minutes of after-walk stretches
FREQUENCY: 3 to 5 times per week
WEEKLY MILEAGE: 12 to 20 miles

5
Walking and Weight Loss

To say that most women in this country consider themselves overweight is an enormous understatement. Few women *don't* think they have a few pounds to shed. Researchers have found that a majority of women perceive their bodies to be heavier than they actually are, and aspire to unhealthful thinness. While women's obsession with weight loss itself is certainly unhealthful, about 16.3 million American women *are significantly* overweight, to an extent that it is a major public health problem.

Weight 20 percent higher than desirable—termed obesity—is associated with several risk factors for heart disease, such as high blood pressure, elevated serum cholesterol and triglycerides, and diabetes. Obesity has also been associated with degenerative joint disease and some cancers—including breast cancer—that are more common in overweight individuals.

While it's long been believed that obesity was caused simply by overeating, we now know that its causes are very complex. There is a growing belief that obesity is caused more by low levels of physical activity than by an increase in food intake.

The value of walking as a weight-loss tool has been vastly underestimated. You might be surprised to hear that if you fitness-walk forty-five minutes a day, four times a week throughout a year, you'll lose eighteen pounds, provided you don't increase your food intake. The loss will be greater if combined with a moderate reduction in calories. One simple way

> **A typical woman uses about 55 calories an hour when she is asleep.**

to lose weight is to go out and take a fitness walk every day during lunch time.

Walking is particularly good if you are extremely overweight, because higher impact activities such as running may be too hard on your bones and joints. The Rockport Fitness Walking Test is just as valid in overweight individuals as it is in individuals at ideal body weight.

If you're planning to include walking in a weight loss program, it's a good idea to know at the start just how overweight—or overfat—you are. Overfat means that while your weight may be acceptable for your size, your fat-to-muscle ratio could be improved. A healthful body fat percentage for women is from 20 to 25 percent. The most accurate way to measure body fat is underwater weighing, but this is expensive and time consuming.

The skinfold technique involves measuring the thickness of the pinched fold of fat at three points on the body. This method is not as accurate as underwater weighing but provides a good estimate of your amount of body fat. Many exercise facilities have staff who are trained in the skinfold technique. Over the course of a long-term exercise program, body fat and body measurements will be a better gauge of progress than pounds. You may lose inches and increase your muscle tone without losing a pound—may even gain slightly, because muscle mass is more dense than fat.

Every woman knows the difficulty of losing weight and not having it find its way back to her, but the principle for effective weight control is actually very simple. To maintain your current weight you need to expend the same number of calories that you consume. To lose weight you need to expend *more* calories than you consume, and to gain weight you consume more calories than you expend. This is called the energy balance equation.

If you want to lose weight, there are three ways of "unbalancing" the equation in your favor:

1. diet—reduce caloric intake;
2. exercise—maintain regular food intake, but increase physical activity;
3. combination—reduce caloric intake and increase physical activity.

It's clear that a combination of exercise and diet works best; to understand why, think of it as a matching funds campaign: every calorie you burn by walking adds value to your reduced caloric intake. For example, a 1200-calorie diet combined with one hour of walking per day is as effective as a 900-calorie diet. This has the advantage of reducing the risk of deficiencies in vitamins, minerals and protein often associated with dieting.

HOW MUCH CAN WALKING HELP?

A number of scientific studies have shown that exercise can make a considerable difference in a weight-loss program. In one particularly interesting study, three groups of eleven overweight women were put on a program designed to achieve a deficit of 500 calories per day. The diet group decreased intake by 500 calories per day with no change in regular exercise; the exercise group burned 500 calories per day with no change in caloric intake, and the exercise-diet group ate 250 calories fewer per day and did 250 calories' worth of exercise. All three groups lost ten to twelve pounds. However, both exercise groups had significantly greater reductions in body fat than did the diet group, and the diet group demonstrated an undesirable loss in lean body weight.

The strongest evidence for the effects of exercise on weight loss comes from a study published in 1979. Three treatments were compared in this study, also: diet alone, exercise alone and a combination of diet and exercise. The diet group lost seven pounds, the exercise group lost six pounds and the combined group lost thirteen pounds. Furthermore, at both eight-week and twenty-four-week follow-ups, the combined group continued to lose weight, whereas the other two groups did not.

WHY WALKING WORKS

Walking, like any form of aerobic exercise, makes four major contributions to your weight-loss program: it increases caloric expenditure, controls appetite, helps maintain resting metabolic rate and burns fat while increasing muscle mass.

The first factor, increased caloric expenditure, is obvious. How walking affects your appetite, however, is not always well understood. There's a dieter's myth that exercise stimulates appetite and increases caloric intake, thus canceling out its benefits. However, there is good evidence to show that regular physical activity of moderate intensity may actually reduce appetite in people who are very sedentary.

In one study, animals whose activities were restricted by confinement in small cages consumed more calories than they needed, and got fat. (It's like eating a bag of M & M's candy when you're bored.) In another study, rats that were exercised moderately a short time each day actually ate less and maintained a lower body weight than sedentary animals.

Similar results have been found in a study of mill workers. The least active workers—who tended to be overweight—consumed almost as many calories as the most active, and approximately 500 calories each day more than the moderately active workers.

Resting metabolic rate (RMR) is the term used for the amount of energy your body burns during rest; RMR goes down as you decrease caloric consumption. Severe caloric restriction may depress your RMR by as much as 45 percent; consequently, you burn fewer calories while at rest and performing usual activities. This decrease in RMR is probably responsible for the plateaus you hit on a diet—even though you're still eating less, you stop losing weight.

Some research data suggests that exercise may help to keep your RMR up while you diet. More research is needed to determine the mechanism involved and how much exercise is needed to maintain RMR, but this is further evidence favoring the diet-walking combo for weight-loss.

Finally, when you go on a diet, up to 40 percent of your weight loss may actually be the loss of protein and muscle mass (lean body weight). Combining an exercise program with a diet reduces the loss of lean body weight and promotes fat loss. You may actually see a small increase in weight, but since it's lean muscle mass, your measurements should decrease, and your jeans should feel looser.

PRESCRIPTION FOR WEIGHT LOSS

If weight control is your ultimate goal, you may want to adjust your walking accordingly. Since your goal is to burn calories, walk more frequently (five to seven days per week), for longer duration (forty-five minutes or more), at a slightly lower intensity (60 to 75 percent of predicted maximum heart rate). By decreasing your pace, you can walk a longer distance without getting tired, and thereby expend more calories. The number of calories you burn on a walk is based on your walking pace, duration or distance and body weight. The table below shows the number of calories burned per mile for walking 3.0 to 4.5 mph for different body weights.

CALORIC COST OF WALKING (CALORIES/MILE)*

Walking Pace (mph)	Body Weight				
	100 lbs.	125 lbs.	150 lbs.	175 lbs.	200 lbs.
			Calories Burned		
3.0	52	66	79	92	105
3.5	54	67	80	94	107
4.0	58	72	87	101	116
4.5	65	81	97	113	129

*Based on Bubb, et al. *Journal of Cardiac Rehabilitation* 5:462–465, 1985.

For a safe and effective weight control program, it is generally recommended that you try to lose no more than one to two pounds per week. For each pound you lose you must expend 3500 calories more than you consume.

To lose one pound per week you need a caloric deficit of 500

About one-third of the weight lost from all types of diets conducted without exercise is lean tissue, not fat tissue.

calories per day. One good way to achieve this is to try to walk about fifteen miles per week (three miles, five days per week, or two miles, seven days per week). This will burn approximately 1000–2000 calories per week depending on your walking pace and body weight (see Caloric Cost of Walking chart). The remaining 200 to 400 calories per day can be easily cut from your diet by skipping snacks and foods high in fats. This method will leave you less hungry and help you maintain your lean body weight while losing fat.

If you think you need to lose a large amount of weight, see your physician first. He or she can first make sure there is no reason you should not go on a weight reduction program, and then possibly recommend exercises and refer you to a dietician for an individualized diet plan.

SPOT REDUCTION

Unfortunately, it's simply not true that if you exercise your stomach, you burn stomach fat. This misconception is the basis for the idea of "spot reduction." Considerable scientific research provides evidence against spot reduction: while some exercises may tone your muscles, making you appear slimmer in that area, any fat loss is distributed throughout your body.

CHOOSING AN EATING PLAN

We've been focusing on the walking half of the exercise-diet combo, but diet is equally important. Most women are familiar with the yo-yo syndrome of fad-diet weight loss: the quick drop of a few pounds, equally quickly put back. It's an unhealthful, frustrating cycle. To break it, you need to develop an eating pattern that you can live with the rest of your life. The next chapter should help you make dietary changes that, when combined with walking, can make you look and feel better.

6
Nutrition for the Woman Fitness Walker

If you're like most women, you try to eat right, but aren't always certain that you do. Sometimes, in fact, you're quite certain that you don't. You try to cut out fats, cholesterol and calories. You think about calcium, iron and other nutrients, and wonder if you get enough. But it's hard to constantly monitor what you eat, and to control every aspect of your diet. Face it, sometimes you're just going to eat what's available—whether it's cheese, crackers and wine or a hamburger and french fries. Still, eating right is a goal worth pursuing—it can make a difference in the way you feel day to day, and help you stay consistently energetic and healthy.

THE DIET-HEALTH-ENERGY CONNECTION

Although many lifestyle factors or habits affect your health, what you eat is one of the most important. Your risk of heart disease, stroke, diabetes, certain cancers and obesity are all affected by your diet. In addition to your overall health, what you eat can also have a dramatic effect on your energy level and your ability to perform daily tasks. Have you ever skipped lunch to find yourself irritable, cranky and unable to concentrate by 3 PM? Conversely, after a very large meal you may feel sleepy and ready for a nap.

What should you eat, then, for optimal energy and prevention of diet-related illness? For starters, begin by incorporating the dietary guidelines set forth by the American Heart Association (AHA) in 1986 into your own goals for improved nutrition. Specific tips to help you get your diet within these somewhat confusing guidelines will follow.

The American Heart Association Dietary Guidelines

1. Saturated fat intake should be less than 10 percent of calories.
2. Total fat intake should be less than 30 percent of calories.
3. Cholesterol intake should be less than 100 mg per 1000 calories, not to exceed 300 mg per day.
4. Protein intake should be approximately 15 percent of calories.
5. Carbohydrate intake should make up 50 to 55 percent or more of calories with emphasis on increasing complex carbohydrates.
6. The sodium intake should be reduced to approximately 1 gram per 1000 calories, not to exceed 3 grams per day.
7. If you drink alcoholic beverages, the limit should be 15 percent of total calories, not to exceed one ounce of alcohol (approximately two drinks) per day.
8. Total calories should be sufficient to maintain the individual's best body weight.
9. A wide variety of foods should be consumed.

Another practical—and somewhat simpler—approach to improved nutrition is called the 80/20 Rule. It simplifies the confusing world of nutrition and works like this: Make sure 80 percent of the food you eat is nourishing and wholesome—low in fat and high in fiber; the other 20 percent of your diet can be whatever you like. Allow yourself—in small amounts—your favorite indulgences: ice cream, brownies or guacamole and chips. By following the 80/20 Rule the foundation of your diet will be solid, so a small amount of less-nutritious food isn't a big deal. (Specific recommendations for using the 80/20 Rule are found at the end of this chapter.)

Now to get down to nutritional nuts and bolts: what foods are your biggest enemies, and how can you avoid them?

ATTACK FAT

Fat in your food is by far the worst offender. It has been conclusively linked to diabetes, heart disease and is a suspected carcinogen. In addition, ounce for ounce, fat has more than *twice* the calories of either carbohydrates or protein. Even if you're careful about avoiding greasy foods and skipping the butter, chances are you eat more fat than you think. The average woman gets about 43 percent of her daily calories as fat: that almost equals the amount of fat in a stick of butter—consumed each day! One reason for this is that over half the fat we eat is hidden in other foods like cheese, cookies and crackers. Even well-trimmed lean meats contain a large dose of hidden fat. To find out if you are eating too much fat, take the Nutricheck test on page 82.

Ideally, you want to cut your fat intake from 43 percent to 30 percent. In addition to reducing the *quantity* of fat you eat, you should also be aware of the *quality* of the fats you are eating.

There are three basic types of fat—saturated, monounsaturated and polyunsaturated. Animal fats tend to be saturated and solid at room temperature, whereas plant or vegetable fats are usually monounsaturated or polyunsaturated and liquid at room temperature. Note, however, that there are two vegetable fats that are quite saturated—palm and coconut oils (see chart, which follows).

Saturated fats tend to raise blood cholesterol levels; monounsaturated fats and polyunsaturated fats may even reduce serum cholesterol. (The higher the blood cholesterol level, the greater the risk of heart disease.) Monounsaturated fats, however, may be best because they tend to lower only the "bad" cholesterol, termed LDL, while polyunsaturated fats lower both the good (HDL) and bad blood cholesterol. The AHA guidelines suggest breaking down fat intake into less than 10 percent saturated fat, less than 10 percent polyunsaturated fat, with the remaining fat coming from the monounsaturates. While controlling these percentages precisely is unrealistic, you can prob-

NUTRICHECK

Circle the appropriate score corresponding to the number of servings per week for each food item.

Food	Serving Size	Servings per Week	Score
Red meat and/or poultry with skin	4 ounces (size of palm of hand)	0–3 4–7 8–11 12–15	5 4 3 2
Fish	4 ounces	0–3 4–7	5 3
Eggs	one	0–4 5–7 8+	2 0 −2
Cheese—full fat (Swiss, cheddar, jack, etc.)	2 ounces (2 cubic inches)	0–2 3–4 5–6 7+	5 3 2 −1
Cheese—low fat (cottage, mozzarella, etc.)	2 ounces (2 cubic inches)	0–3 4–7	5 3
Milk, yogurt—full fat	8 ounces (1 cup)	0–2 3–4 5–6	5 3 2
Milk, yogurt—skim or low fat	8 ounces	0–7 8–15	5 1
Legumes (beans)	4 ounces (½ cup)	1–3 4–7	6 10
Fruit	1 piece	1–3 4–7 8–11 12–15	3 5 7 9
Vegetables	4 ounces (½ cup)	1–3 4–7 8–11 12–15	3 5 7 9

Salad greens	small bowl	1–3	2
		4–7	3
		8–11	4
		12–15	5
Whole grain breads & cereals (whole wheat or oatmeal bread, granola, oatmeal cereal, etc.)	1 slice/bowl	1–3	2
		4–7	3
		8–11	4
		12–15	5
Crackers and chips	10–15	0–1	3
		2–3	2
		4–5	−1
		6–7(+)	−3
Sweets: cakes, doughnuts, pie, cookies, candy	1 piece 2 pieces	0–1	3
		2–3	2
		4–5	−1
		6–7	−3
Butter, margarine, oils (salad dressings, mayonnaise, oil used in cooking)	2 Tbsp.	0–14	5
		15–20	3
		21–28	−1

TOTAL SCORE:
(add numbers circled) _____

Perfect Score: 80 (Nutriwork's 80/20 Rule)

Score	Risk of Heart Disease Due to Diet	% of Diet as Fat (Approximate)
80–70	Very low	25
70–60	Low	32
60–50	Average*	40
50–40	High	45
40–30 or under	Very high	50

*If you scored 55 or below, your diet contains the amount of fat in the average American diet—about 40% fat, far above the amount recommended by the American Heart Association.

Source: Kapitan, R.: The Newtrition Workshop.

	Saturated Fats	Monounsaturated Fats	Polyunsaturated Fats
most saturated	ANIMAL SOURCES • cheese • butter • milk • meat • eggs • lard • pork PLANT SOURCES • coconut oil • palm oil • chocolate	ANIMAL SOURCES • chicken • fish PLANT SOURCES • vegetable shortening • avocados • pecans • olive oil • stick margarine • peanut oil • peanut butter • cottonseed oil	PLANT SOURCES • almonds • walnuts • filberts • soft margarine • sesame oil • mayonnaise • soybean oil • corn oil • sunflower oil • safflower oil

least saturated

Food	Portion	Average Mg Cholesterol
Egg	1	250
Liver, cooked	1 ounce	125
Shrimp, cooked	1 ounce	40
Milk, whole	1 cup	30
Cheese (cheddar or jack)	1 ounce	30
Crab or lobster, cooked	1 ounce	25
Beef, pork or lamb, cooked	1 ounce	25
Poultry, cooked	1 ounce	25
Fish, cooked	1 ounce	20
Clams or oysters, cooked	1 ounce	20
Butter	1 teaspoon	10
Mayonnaise	1 teaspoon	5
Legumes, cooked	1 cup	0
Peanuts	1 handful	0
Rice, oats or pasta, cooked	1 cup	0
Fruit	1 cup	0
Vegetable	1 cup	0

ably improve your diet simply by trying to use more monounsaturates and polyunsaturates, while cutting back on saturated fat.

From the chart at left it is easy to see how to cut down your intake of animal saturated fats. Saturated plant fats—coconut and palm oils in particular—come from less obvious sources. It's important to read the label of the packaged, processed food you buy to determine the type of fat used. Many dessert foods like cakes, pies, puddings, pastries and cookies, as well as chips, crackers, breads and other bakery products, are full of saturated vegetable fats. In fact, ounce for ounce, chocolate chip cookies contain *more* saturated fat than a T-bone steak.

In addition to cutting back on total and saturated fat intake, try to limit cholesterol to 300 mg a day or less (see preceding chart.)

NINE FAT-FIGHTING TIPS

1. Eat small, lean cuts of red meat trimmed of visible fat and try to eat no more than two servings of red meat a week. A typical serving is eight to ten ounces—about the size of your hand; a smaller portion would be three to four ounces. Good choices: broiled meats—sirloin, round flank, veal, lean ground beef. Poor choices: cheeseburgers, prime rib, T-bone steak, chuck roast and other fatty cuts.
2. Try to avoid high-fat processed meats like bacon, luncheon meats, sausage, corned beef and frankfurters.
3. Remove the skin from poultry before cooking to reduce its fat calories by one-half.
4. Substitute low-fat fish, bean or poultry dishes for red meat.
5. Prepare meats, poultry, fish and beans with minimal fat. Good choices: baked, broiled, roasted in its own juice. Poor choices: fried, served with fatty gravies or cream and/or cheese sauces.
6. Substitute low-fat dairy foods for full-fat varieties. Good choices: skim or low-fat milk and yogurt, low-fat cottage cheese, part-skim mozzarella, ricotta and Swiss cheeses. Poor choices: whole milk, full-fat or artificial cheeses—American, cheddar, Havarti, Brie, cream cheese, etc.
7. Read labels and watch for palm and/or coconut oil in cakes, cookies, crackers, pies and pastries.

8. Stay away from fried and high-fat foods—fried fish, chicken, french fries, chips (potato, corn, taco, etc.).
9. Prepare foods with minimal fat and avoid using vegetable shortening—a hydrogenated fat. Use a combination of one part butter/one part safflower oil in preparing a food that calls for butter, margarine or vegetable shortening. Add one-half the amount of fat called for in a recipe for an entree; in most cases it will not affect the final product.

FIBER FITNESS

Most women stand to gain from boosting their fiber intake. In fact, fiber and fat have an inverse relationship—high-fiber foods are usually low in fat and vice versa. So, if you rated poorly in terms of your fat intake on the Nutricheck test, chances are you're not eating enough high-fiber foods. The average woman eats four pounds of food a day; three of them come from meat, cheese, poultry, fish, eggs, sugar, fats and beverages—all of which are relatively high in fat and low in fiber. The four types of food high in fiber are whole grains, fruits, vegetables and legumes (beans).

One reason why women don't get enough fiber is that the convenient processed foods we turn to on a hectic day are usually lacking in fiber content.

There are basically two kinds of fiber: insoluble and water soluble. Boosting your intake of fiber, particularly the insoluble kind, will help reduce symptoms of chronic constipation. Insoluble fiber absorbs water from the gastrointestinal tract, making stools bulkier and softer, and elimination easier and faster. Good sources of insoluble fiber are wheat bran and the outer husks of other whole grains (barley, rye, etc.), and certain vegetables like broccoli, peppers and cabbage.

Insoluble fiber has also been linked to a reduction in the risk of developing colon cancer; however, more research is needed to understand exactly how this works.

Consumption of soluble fiber has been found to decrease the level of blood cholesterol, thus lowering the risk of coronary heart disease, although the mechanism is unclear. Good sources of soluble fiber are oatmeal, legumes, fruit and certain vegetables.

Adding bran flakes to a highly processed low-fiber diet might be the easiest way to increase your fiber intake, but it's not the best. There are many varieties of fiber within the two basic categories of water soluble and insoluble, and it's best to eat a wide variety of high-fiber foods of all four types.

To find out if you are eating enough fiber-rich foods, write down everything you eat for the next three days. Then add up the grams of fiber and refer to the scoreboard on page 88. While there is no specific recommendation for fiber, at least 25 grams of fiber a day is a healthful goal; most women eat between five and ten grams.

EATING MORE WHOLE GRAINS

One of the best ways to boost your fiber intake is to eat more whole grains—foods like wheat, corn, barley, rye and oats in their whole form. Most of the grains we eat are refined: part or all of the original components of the grain are removed and, ironically, fed to farm animals for their rich nutrient content.

In the making of refined wheat (white) flour from whole wheat, the bran (goodbye, fiber) and the germ (goodbye, minerals and vitamins E and B) are removed. Even though most white flour is enriched, only four of the original fourteen nutrients removed are added back; and only one-fourth the fiber remains.

The easiest way to eat more whole grains is to eat whole wheat bread and bread products. Don't assume that a bread is whole grain just because it's dark in color—"tinted bread," as it is commonly called, can fool the eye.

To determine whether or not a bread is truly whole wheat, first give it the squeeze test. Remember squishing white bread into little tiny balls when you were a kid? Well, whole wheat bread is more hearty and firmer than white bread, so it doesn't squish. Next, read the label. If it doesn't say *whole* wheat (or rye, corn, etc.) flour, it can technically be white flour.

Breads that contain a 50/50 blend of whole and refined grain are better than white bread, but not so nutritious as 100 percent whole grain. A 50/50 bread is a good place to start if you or your family have a hard time adjusting to the flavor and consistency of 100 percent whole grain bread.

Other ways to boost your fiber intake include switching to brown rice or whole wheat pasta, choosing whole grain or bran cereals, and trying whole grains like cracked wheat or kasha (buckwheat) as a side dish instead of white rice, instant mashed potatoes or french fries.

FIBER SCOREBOARD

Food	Amount	Gms Fiber
Fresh Fruit (raw or cooked, w/ skin)		
Apples, pears, berries	1 piece or ¹/₂ cup	4.0
All others	1 piece or ¹/₂ cup	1.5
Canned Fruit (w/o skin)	¹/₂ cup	1.5
Dried Fruit	¹/₂ cup	4.0
Fresh Vegetables (raw or cooked)		
Peas, parsnips	¹/₂ cup	5.0
Potatoes	1 baked w/skin	4.0
Corn, squash, tomatoes	¹/₂ cup	2.0
Cabbage family, carrots	¹/₂ cup	2.0
All others	¹/₂ cup	1.5
Tossed Salad Greens	1 cup	1.5
Cereal: Cooked whole grain	¹/₂ cup	2.5
Bran types	¹/₂ cup	4.0
Granola, whole grain	¹/₂ cup	2.5
Refined	¹/₂ cup	1.0
Bread: Whole grain	1 slice	2.5
Refined	1 slice	1.0
Bran muffin	1 muffin	3.0
Crackers: Whole grain	3 rye wafers/6 small	2.5
Graham crackers	2 squares	1.5
Refined	6 small	.5
Popcorn	1 cup	3.0
Pasta, Rice: Whole Grain	1 cup cooked	3.0
Refined	1 cup cooked	1.0
Nuts, Seeds	¹/₄ cup, 2 oz.	5.0
Legumes	¹/₂ cup	6.0
Meat, Cheese, Fats, Most Sweets		0

Source: Kapitan, R.: The Newtrition Workshop

STRATEGIES FOR EATING MORE WHOLE GRAINS

Replace This	*with This*
White rice	brown rice
	bulgar pilaf
	kasha
	millet pilaf
Saltines, cheese crackers, onion crackers, etc.	whole grain wheat, rye or rice crackers
Presweetened breakfast cereals	whole grain cereals, granola
White bread	whole grain breads, English muffins or bagels
White baking flour	50/50 whole wheat/white in cookies, piecrust, oatmeal cookies
Potato chips	popcorn
Glazed doughnut, pastry	bran, blueberry or corn muffin

CALCIUM COUNTS

Osteoporosis and calcium . . . they've been on almost as many magazine covers as Cybill Shepherd and Bruce Willis. Unfortunately, much of this media hype came too late for many women whose diets lacked calcium when it was most needed. But much that every woman should know has been learned about calcium and osteoporosis.

Osteoporosis is a bone-thinning disease that primarily afflicts older women. Bone is an active substance; it undergoes constant remodeling throughout life. It may begin to degenerate in a woman as early as age twenty to thirty, and after menopause when the production of estrogen decreases, the rate of bone loss increases significantly. Risk factors associated with the onset of osteoporosis in women, in descending order of importance, are:

• Caucasian race (particularly fair-skinned and of northern European descent)

- low weight for height
- early menopause (natural or induced, e.g., hysterectomy)
- post menopause
- sedentary lifestyle
- calcium deficiency
- family history of osteoporosis
- excessive smoking or drinking; excessive consumption of coffee or tea (more than five cups daily)

Women are at greater risk of developing osteoporosis than men for several reasons. Women start off at a disadvantage, having 30 percent less bone mass than men, and women generally eat fewer calories (and less calcium) than men, yet have the same or greater calcium requirement.

Prevention and Treatment

The goal of both prevention and treatment of osteoporosis is to increase bone mass. The safest way to do this is to combine regular exercise with an adequate calcium intake. Weight-bearing exercise, like walking, promotes the formation of new bone, and calcium is the mineral from which it is made.

In addition to regular walking, try to eat enough calcium-rich foods. Milk and dairy products are probably the first foods you think of, but certain vegetables (broccoli and cauliflower), beans, grains, fish with edible bones, such as like sardines, and some fruits are high in calcium.

The female hormone estrogen has been used experimentally to slow osteoporosis. Estrogen therapy, however, is not without risks—some high-dose regimens have been associated with increased risk of breast and endometrial cancer. More research is needed to determine its safety and effectiveness.

If you're wondering whether or not you need to boost your calcium intake, write down everything you eat for a three-day period, then check the calcium content of each item in the chart which follows and calculate your totals for the day. The Recommended Daily Allowance (RDA) of calcium for women is 800 mg; 1200 mg if you're pregnant or lactating.

If you're relying heavily on dairy products for your calcium quota, you'll want to make your choices low in fat, in keeping with your other dietary goals.

NATURALLY RICH SOURCES OF CALCIUM

Food	Serving Size	Calcium (mgs)
DAIRY		
Milk		
skim	1 cup	298
low-fat	1 cup	297
buttermilk	1 cup	296
whole	1 cup	288
chocolate	1 cup	280
evaporated	1 cup	1034
noninstant, nonfat		
dry milk powder	¼ cup	392
Cream, light	1 cup	259
Cheese		
ricotta, part-skim	½ cup	337
Parmesan	1 oz.	320
Gruyère	1 oz.	308
Swiss	1 oz.	272
cheddar	1 oz.	211
muenster	1 oz.	203
mozzarella	1 oz.	183
American	1 oz.	174
cream	1 Tbsp.	139
cottage cheese, creamed	½ cup	105
dry curd	½ cup	77
Cheez Whiz	1 Tbsp.	75
Ice cream	½ cup	97
Ice milk	½ cup	274
Yogurt	1 cup	270–293
NONDAIRY		
Breads		
Muffins		
bran	1 medium	142
corn	1 medium	105
Buttermilk pancakes	3–4	174
Tortilla	1	60
White or whole wheat bread	2 slices	48
Desserts, Flavorings		
Kelp	1 tsp.	93
Molasses, blackstrap	1 Tbsp.	116
Maple syrup	1 Tbsp.	33
Carob flour	3.5 oz./100 mg	352

Pudding

baked custard	$^1/_2$ cup	150
vanilla, homemade	$^1/_2$ cup	144
chocolate, from mix	$^1/_2$ cup	187
Frozen yogurt, fruit flavor	$^1/_2$ cup	100
Cheesecake, Sara Lee	1 piece	88

Entrees

Welsh rarebit	1 cup	582
Macaroni and cheese	1 cup	362
Cheese souffle	1 cup	300
Lasagna	1 cup	252
Clam chowder, New England style	1 cup	240
Bean burrito	1 avg.	208
Tuna and noodles	1 cup	194
Pizza	1 piece	156

Fish

Sardines, with bones	8 med.	354
Mackerel, canned	4 oz.	208
Salmon, with bones	3 oz.	167
Oysters	3 oz. (7–9)	113
Shrimp, canned	3 oz.	99
Haddock	4 oz.	45
Flounder	4 oz.	25

Fruits

Figs, dried	4 large	160
Dates, pitted	1 cup	105
Apricots, dried	1 cup	101
Rhubarb	1 cup, cooked, raw	96
Watermelon	4" x 8" piece	65
Orange	1 medium	54
Blackberries	1 cup	46

Grains

Amaranth	1 cup, cooked	178
Buckwheat	1 cup, cooked	85
Rye	1 cup, cooked	26
Oatmeal	1 cup, cooked	21
Rice, brown	1 cup, cooked	18
Wheat, whole grain	1 cup, cooked	17
Wheat germ	1 Tbsp.	7
Popcorn	1 cup, popped	2

Legumes

Kidney beans, cooked	1$^1/_2$ cups	204
Navy beans	1$^1/_2$ cups	150
Tofu	4 oz.	150
Soybeans, cooked	$^1/_2$ cup	66
Soybean milk	1$^1/_2$ cups	18

Nuts and Seeds

Brazil nuts	$^1/_4$ cup	140
Almonds, filberts	$^1/_4$ cup	80
Peanuts	$^1/_4$ cup	45
Pecans	$^1/_4$ cup	20
Sunflower seeds	$^1/_4$ cup	45
Sesame seeds	$^1/_4$ cup	40

Vegetables
Cooked

collard greens	$^1/_2$ cup	179
turnip greens	$^1/_2$ cup	133
dandelion greens	$^1/_2$ cup	140
bok choy	$^1/_2$ cup	126
kale	$^1/_2$ cup	103
mustard greens	$^1/_2$ cup	138
beet greens	$^1/_2$ cup	119
artichoke	1 large	102
green beans	1 cup	99
okra	8–9 pods	92
spinach	$^1/_2$ cup	83
sweet potato	1 large baked	72
rutabaga	$^1/_2$ cup mashed	71
lima beans	1 cup	55

Raw

watercress	1 cup chopped	189
parsley	1 cup chopped	114
Swiss chard	1 cup	110

Calcium contents drawn from: Pennington, Jean A., and Church, Helen N., *Food Values of Portions Commonly Used.* New York: Harper and Row, 1985; and U.S. Department of Agriculture, *Nutritive Value of American Food*, Agriculture Handbook 456, 1975.

Calcium Supplements

Most women get about 500 mg per day of calcium from the food they eat, so many have turned to supplements to boost their intake. There is no consensus among health professionals about the adequacy and safety of taking supplements. With careful planning, you can derive all the calcium you need from your diet, but if you want to use supplements, make sure the calcium is in one of two easily absorbed forms—calcium carbonate or calcium lactate. (Steer clear of the latter if you have lactose intolerance.) A daily supplement of between 300 mg and 800 mg is considered safe.

IRON

Iron is the mineral that aids in oxygen transport in your blood. When your muscles are working hard, as in fitness walking, their oxygen requirements increase dramatically. A deficiency of iron, therefore, may interfere with your body's ability to supply enough oxygen to working muscles.

Most women get about 6 mg of iron for each 1000 calories they eat. Since the average daily caloric intake for women is 1800 calories, that equals about 11 mg; yet the RDA for this nutrient is 18 mg a day (for menstruating women). To boost your iron intake, choose at least two servings of high-iron foods a day. Although both animal and vegetable foods contain iron, the iron in animal foods is more easily absorbed. You can boost the absorption of iron in vegetable foods by eating them with a food high in vitamin C (such as orange juice or potatoes). The starred iron sources below are naturally high in vitamin C.

FOOD SOURCES: IRON

Food	Amount	Iron (mgs)
Egg	1	1.1
Hamburger	3 oz.	3.0
Chili and beans	1 cup	4.2
Liver	4 oz.	3.0
Oysters	½ cup	6.6
Sardines	3 oz.	2.5

Food	Amount	Iron (mgs)
Shrimp	3 oz.	2.6
Almonds (shelled)	½ cup	3.4
Dry beans, cooked	½ cup	2.8
Black walnuts (shelled)	½ cup	3.8
*Collard greens	1 cup	1.1
*Dandelion greens	1 cup	3.2
*Green peas	½ cup	2.1
*Mustard greens	1 cup	2.5
Hot peppers (dried)	1 tablespoon	2.3
*Green pepper	1	.4
*Spinach	1 cup	4.7
*Tomato juice	1 cup	2.2
*Apricots (dried)	½ cup	4.1
*Cantaloupe	½	.8
Dates	½ cup	2.6
Dried figs	1	.6
Dried peaches	½ cup	4.8
Prunes (dried)	4	1.1
Prune juice	1 cup	10.5
Raisins	½ cup	2.4
Blackstrap molasses	1 tablespoon	3.2

Cooking foods in cast iron will boost their iron content, especially foods high in vitamin C (e.g., tomato sauce).

AN EATING PLAN FOR WOMEN FITNESS WALKERS

The 80/20 approach to nutrition assigns food to three categories based on nutritional qualities: 80 percent foods provide maximum nutrition and 20 percent foods provide minimal nutrition. The table below provides examples of foods found in each of these three categories.

NUTRIWORK'S 80/20 EATING GUIDE

80% Foods *ANYTIME* Everyday	50% Foods *IN MODERATION* 3 times/week	20% Foods *NOW AND THEN* Once a week
Protein Foods (2 servings per day) Chicken, Cornish hen or turkey, broiled, boiled, baked or roasted (no skin) (no fatty sauces) Dried beans and peas (legumes) Lean fish:	Chicken, Cornish hen or turkey, broiled, boiled baked or roasted (with skin) Chicken liver Eggs, whole Fatty fish:	Beef liver Cheese omelet Duck, goose Fast foods Fried chicken Ground beef Ham, trimmed Lox Most frozen dinners Nuts, oil roasted and salted Processed meats:
bass red snapper cod rockfish flounder sole haddock tuna, water-packed perch white fish pollock Shellfish	bluefish salmon mackerel swordfish halibut tuna, oil-packed Fried fish Ground round Lamb Nuts, raw or dry roasted Peanut, almond or sesame butter Pork shoulder or loin, lean Round, sirloin, flank steak Rump roast Seeds: sunflower, sesame, pumpkin Tofu, tempeh Veal	bacon bologna corned beef hot dogs liverwurst salami sausage Red meats, untrimmed Spareribs

Dairy Products (3 to 4 servings per day for children, 2 for adults)

Buttermilk (skim)
Low-fat cottage cheese
Low-fat milk (1%)
Low-fat yogurt
Nonfat dry milk
Skim milk
Skim milk and fruit shake
Skim milk cheeses:
  mozzarella, part-skim
  ricotta, part-skim

Cocoa with skim milk
Cottage cheese, regular
Ice milk
Low-fat milk (2%)
Medium-fat cheeses:
  Swiss
  brie
  romano
  mozzarella
Yogurt:
  low-fat, sweetened
  whole milk
  frozen

Cheesecake
Cheese fondue
Cheese soufflé
Eggnog
Hard cheeses:
  blue   cheddar
  brick   muenster
Ice cream
Processed cheeses:
  American
  Velveeta
Quiche
Whole milk

Breads, Grains, Cereals (4 or more servings per day)

Breads and muffins, whole grain
Crackers, whole grain nonfat
Pasta, whole wheat
Sprouts
Whole grain hot and cold cereals
Whole grains:
  barley   rice, brown
  buckwheat   rye
  couscous   triticale
  bulgur (cracked wheat)
  oatmeal, steel-cut oats
  millet
Whole wheat matzoh

Cereals, refined, unsweetened
Cornbread
Crackers, refined, low-fat
Flour tortilla/chapati
Granola cereals
Hominy grits
Pizza
Waffles or pancakes, whole grain
  with minimal sweetener
White bread and rolls
White matzoh
White pasta
Whole grain cakes/cookies

Cakes
Cereals, presweetened
Chips, potato/tortilla
Cookies
Crackers, refined, fatty type
Croissant
Doughnut
Pastries, snack foods
Pies
Sticky buns
Stuffing (with butter)
Waffles or pancakes from refined
  flour with syrup and added fat

80% Foods *ANYTIME* Everyday	50% Foods *IN MODERATION* 3 times/week	20% Foods *NOW AND THEN* Once a week
Fruits and Vegetables (6 or more servings per day)		
All fruits and vegetables except those at right	Avocado, guacamole	Coconut
Applesauce, unsweetened	Coleslaw	Cranberry sauce, canned
Dried fruit	Fruits canned without syrup	French fries
Potatoes, white or sweet	Fruit juices, sweetened	Fruits canned with syrup
Unsalted vegetable juices	Potatoes, au gratin, hash browns	Pickles
Unsweetened fruit juices	Salted vegetable juices	Vegetables canned with salt;
	Vegetables: canned w/o salt frozen, plain	frozen with cream sauce

The Newtrition Workshop, Roxanne Kapitan, chart published by The Network, 1985.

CONCLUSION

"Taking medicine once disease has taken hold is like forging your sword while the battle rages around you."

Chinese Proverb

Taking the time to eat well is a sound investment in yourself. The payoff can be enormous—improved health and performance—and one from which you'll benefit for the rest of your life.

Drink water often during fitness walks; thirst is a *poor* indicator of when you need to drink fluids.

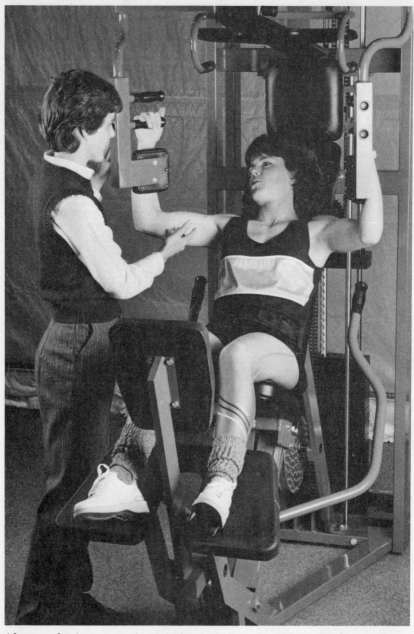

Always obtain proper instruction prior to starting a weight training program. Here Anne discusses her weight training regimen with Sharon Wilkie, who is a certified weight training instructor. *Photo: David Brownell*

7
Muscular Strength and Endurance

So far we've talked mainly about cardiovascular fitness—attained through aerobic exercises like fitness walking. Aerobic capacity and endurance aren't the only measures of fitness, however: muscle strength—the amount of work the muscle can do in an all-out effort—and muscular endurance—the ability of a muscle to maintain a contraction or series of contractions over time— are important as well.

Unfortunately, for most women the term strength training conjures up images of bulging muscles and sweaty gyms. This is a misconception: it's possible for women to do strength train- ing that will result in essentially no change in muscle size, but will improve muscular tone and muscular endurance. In fact, the hormones necessary for muscle enlargement are found in very small quantities in women—well below the level necessary for increases in muscle size.

By developing muscular strength and endurance, you'll be able to perform more efficiently, with less fatigue, and the ben- efits of muscle tone don't need to be explained. Women, in particular, need to work on upper body strength. Research has shown that leg strength is about equal for men and women after adjusting for body size difference, but men's upper bodies are about 30 percent stronger. Apparently, the weight-bearing activity that we do acts as lower body weight training exercises for both sexes. Women's upper bodies, it seems, spend most of the time "going along for the ride," whereas men generally do more upper body exercise.

Strength training can be done at a local health club, or it can be done at home with a small amount of equipment. In fact, certain cardiovascular exercises, like walking with hand-held weights, swimming, cross-country skiing and rowing do have an upper body resistance component that may aid in maintaining upper body strength. If you're seriously interested in developing your strength potential, part of your exercise time should be devoted exclusively to strength-related exercises.

There are many different types of strength training equipment available, each claiming to offer maximum benefits, but research has shown that *how* you work out, and not with what, makes the difference. It's important to understand the principles of strength training; then you'll be ready to do basic exercises to supplement your cardiovascular conditioning program.

The following factors should be considered when designing a muscle strength/endurance program.

Warm-up:	Be sure to spend five to ten minutes stretching before each workout, focusing on the muscle groups that will be used during the workout.
Frequency:	Two to three times per week; weight training can be done on your walking days or on the alternate days. It should never be done two days in a row, although some women save time by doing upper body weights one day, lower body the next.
Instruction:	If you're inexperienced in weight training, seek proper instruction prior to starting a weight training program. A fitness expert at your local health club or recreation facility can generally instruct you on the proper technique and starting weights for developing a safe, effective program. However, men are not always aware of women's fitness needs and abilities, and may prescribe a program that's either too easy or too hard. To be sure you're doing what's right for you, keep the following intensity guidelines in mind.
Intensity:	This refers to both the amount of weight being lifted and the number of repetitions (called reps

in weightlifting lingo). For most women a balanced approach where both strength and endurance are emphasized is best. The weights selected for each exercise should permit you to complete eight to fourteen repetitions. In other words, select a starting weight that you can lift eight to fourteen times while maintaining proper form. If you're mainly interested in toning muscles, aim for high reps. Many women labor, quite literally, under the false belief that greater gain comes from higher weights. In fact, the greatest gain in endurance and tone is made by lifting moderate weights with greater frequency. Two to three sets of eight to fourteen reps is optimal. If you are a beginner start with lighter weights and fewer reps for the first two weeks of your program to reduce your risk of injury and to minimize muscle soreness. A good gauge of appropriate weight load is that you can control the weight without strain, raising and lowering it with a slow, controlled motion.

Progressive Overload: As you get stronger and can do the workout with less fatigue, you'll want to increase the intensity by gradually increasing the reps and/or weight load. Again, only advance to a slightly higher weight load (five pounds higher), one that you can control. Generally, if you can easily do three sets of fourteen repetitions, you're ready to move on.

Exercise Order: Arrange the order of exercise so that muscle groups being trained are not the same as the muscle groups being trained in the previous exercise. In other words, if one exercise works your biceps (upper arms), next work another area, like your quadriceps (legs).

Cool-down: Be sure to stretch for five to ten minutes following your workout to maintain flexibility.

Studies show that weight training in women results in dramatic strength gains with very small increase in muscle size.

Table 7.1 summarizes selected guidelines for muscular conditioning.

TABLE 7.1: GUIDELINES FOR MUSCLE FITNESS DEVELOPMENT

Type	Sets	Reps	Frequency
Strength	2–3	6	2–3 x/wk
Strength/Endurance	2–3	8–10	2–3 x/wk
Endurance	2–3	13–14	2–3 x/wk

To minimize risk of injury, follow these rules:

1. Seek proper instruction;
2. Warm up and cool down by stretching;
3. Breathe regularly during all phases of the exercise;
4. Progress slowly;
5. Use proper body mechanics (proper form)—if you have trouble maintaining your form, you are lifting too much weight;
6. Use consistent rhythm during the set and do not pause between reps.

The eight exercises listed below are examples of the kinds of strength training you can do to enhance your walking program. A book on strength training or a fitness instructor can show you many others for toning specific muscles in your body.

Exercises	Muscle Groups
1. bench press	1. shoulder flexors, elbow extensors
2. leg extension	2. knee extensors
3. bent knee sit-up	3. trunk flexors
4. arm curl	4. elbow flexors
5. leg curl	5. knee flexors
6. upright rowing	6. shoulder abductors and elbow flexors
7. toe raise	7. calf muscles
8. triceps	8. elbow extensors

WALKING WITH BODY WEIGHTS

Recently attention has been given to carrying weights with the arms or on the legs as a way of increasing the intensity and caloric cost of walking. The interest in this topic extends to the scientific community. At a recent national meeting of the American College of Sports Medicine six laboratories presented data regarding various aspects of carrying weights while walking. The papers presented often found varying and often contradictory results.

For the individual starting a fitness walking program, carrying weights either on the arms or on the legs is probably not advisable. Biomechanics studies show that there is a delicate balance between the arms and legs while fitness walking. Weighting either arms or legs may throw off this balance, and possibly strain the elbow, shoulder, hip, knee or ankle joints. Finally, there is some concern and some recent data to suggest that carrying weights in the hands while walking may elevate blood pressure during the exercise.

If you want to increase calories burned while walking, you need to consider where you carry the weight. Carrying hand-held weights at the side or wearing a weighted backpack does not significantly increase caloric cost unless you carry 20 to 30 percent of your body weight (25 to 38 pounds for a 125-pound woman). For most people, carrying this much weight is uncomfortable and leads to a decrease in walking speed.

In some cases, however, walking with weights may be effective. Swinging the arms while carrying light weights does increase caloric cost, and is not inadvisable *as long as the arm swing is a controlled movement.* If you have shoulder, back, neck or elbow problems you should check with your physician before attempting this.

If you're training for racewalking, swinging light weights in your arms while standing still can help build the upper body strength and endurance necessary for higher speeds.

If you already have a high level of muscular fitness, it may be reasonable to carry small two- to five-pound weights as an adjunct to fitness walking. This will build muscular strength; if your goal is to increase the aerobic intensity of walking, it is safer and more effective to increase your walking speed instead.

Finally, weighted backpacks may have a potential role in improving your ability to participate in activities such as backpacking and hiking, and may also strengthen your back muscles.

"I feel very lucky to be able to share in any way my knowledge, understanding and especially my personal experience with the advanced aging process. Believe it or not—it does happen to everyone who has avoided or survived bodily assaults by accidents, illness or ignorance. It isn't aging that is bad for us, it's how we handle it. I, for one, am going to walk with it and enjoy it."
—Molley Yeaton, seventy-five-year-old fitness walker. *Photo: David Brownell*

8
Walking for Older Women

In one sense, it's wrong to have a chapter for women over 50 or 60 or any given age, for that matter. Age is not a determining factor: if you're 60 and have been active all your life, you may have a better outlook toward exercise than a 30-year-old lifelong couch potato. Older women can reap the same benefits from exercise as their daughters and granddaughters, and have the same problems of motivation to overcome. Yet, older women do have some special needs and concerns. The point of this chapter is to encourage older women, especially, to be physically active in the safest, most rewarding way.

Research has shown conclusively that age doesn't have to be a barrier to fitness. At the U/Mass Medical School, a study of individuals ages 70 to 79 found short-term training benefits from fitness walking to be comparable to those of younger individuals. These findings are reflected in the Rockport Fitness Walking Test, which offers a gauge of fitness for women up to age 80. Of course, this doesn't mean you can't exercise after 80—there just weren't enough test subjects in this age range for whom to create a separate category.

So while there is no reason for older women not to walk, there are plenty of reasons why walking becomes an even more ideal form of exercise as you get older. To begin with, much research has shown that participation in regular physical activity is associated with a reduction in the incidence of several chronic degenerative diseases associated with aging: osteoporosis, heart disease, high blood pressure and diabetes. Walking can help prevent the ravages of osteoporosis and offers minimal risk of joint injury.

Aside from these health advantages, the simplicity of walking is an enormous attraction when learning new skills seems more an obstacle than a challenge. Finally, for many older women, the social aspects of walking with friends is a great motivator.

GETTING STARTED

Initiating a walking program for a woman over the age of 50 is really no different than for a younger individual. However, a few precautions are advisable: 1) get clearance from your physician before starting; 2) take the Rockport Fitness Walking Test described in Chapter 3 to establish your baseline fitness level; 3) select the proper fitness walking program described in Chapter 4; 4) always include proper warm-up and cool-down periods to minimize the risk of injury.

How can you expect getting in shape to change the aging process? A number of research studies have recently addressed this issue.

IMPROVED METABOLISM AND WEIGHT CONTROL. · Since resting metabolism decreases with age (you burn fewer calories at rest), walking three to five days per week can be helpful in maintaining body weight. If your walking program is used in conjunction with a sensible diet plan, the additional energy expenditure may help in weight reduction.

MAINTENANCE OF FITNESS LEVELS. · Ten years ago, it was believed that a *normal* consequence of aging was a decline in physical fitness; however, recent studies suggest that the decline in physical fitness is due to decreased physical activity. Thus, if you maintain an active lifestyle and exercise on a *regular* basis, you can maintain better fitness, longer.

It has been estimated that 50 percent of the decline in biological functions between the ages of 30 and 70 is due to disuse.

SLOWING THE PROCESS OF OSTEOPOROSIS. • Fitness walking is one of the simplest, yet most effective types of weight-bearing exercise. The weight-bearing nature of walking puts mechanical stress on the bone that permits more calcium to be taken up by the bone and increases the strength of the bone.

SPECIAL CONSIDERATIONS FOR THE OVER-50 FITNESS WALKER

Equipment

Even though fitness walking is a very low impact sport, it still results in some jarring of the bones and joints. Since ligaments become stiffer with age and cartilage becomes thinner, it is particularly important for you to purchase well-designed, properly padded shoes specifically for fitness walking (see Chapter 2).

Outdoor walking events have become increasingly popular such as this spring event in Washington, D.C., which attracted several hundred walkers, here led by Anne Kashiwa. *Photo: Warren Mattox*

Mall Walking

There is an age-related decline in the ability to dissipate heat during exercise, so if you're older, you need to be cautious about walking in extremes of temperature (either very hot or very cold). One of the activities that has recently gained in popularity among older enthusiasts is walking in climate-controlled shopping malls. All over the country, mall operators are opening their doors early, before regular shopping hours, and inviting walkers to put in a few miles before breakfast. Often sponsored by local hospitals, many malls have walkers' clubs. The social dimension is an added attraction for older walkers—after a few laps among the department stores, it's pleasant to sit down together for coffee and snacks.

Medications

Another consideration for older walkers is the influence of medications on walking, and especially Beta blockers, which are commonly prescribed for individuals who have either high blood pressure or angina. If you take these drugs, see Chapter 10, "Walking for Rehabilitation," for important information.

> **The number of women over 65 exceeds the number of teenage girls in the United States.**

9
Walking and Pregnancy

I began my fitness walking program when I was pregnant with Hennie. I had all the right motives, of course; controlling my weight, keeping my heart in good working order and, most of all, keeping my sanity.

It was time to find out if walking was all it was cracked up to be. At the time there were few fitness walkers on the streets, but being shy was never part of my character. It was a little nasty that February morning, so I slid into my slightly tight sweat pants and turtleneck before starting off.

For the first couple of blocks, I thought there was no way walking would keep me from turning into a butterball; then it occurred to me that if I just exerted myself a little more and used my arms more vigorously, I might be able to go faster. You're probably thinking "but didn't you get those looks?" Well, yes I did, but I felt good about my new walking routine and didn't mind.

The following day, I purchased a book on walking and I've never turned back. From that day in February through the end of my pregnancy, to the day of this writing, I have remained an avid walker. My style is a little cramped lately, however, by the two-year-old who sways happily on my back.

My particular statistics for that pregnancy were average. I gained about thirty-two pounds and delivered an eight-pound, three-ounce boy. The benefits of my activities showed up not in these numbers, however, but in my quick recovery from a Caesarean section and a *return to prepregnancy weight in six months. The importance of this postpregnancy recovery cannot be emphasized enough. Not only can you return to normal activities sooner, but that extra strength helps when it comes time to move a little person and all his personal items. A good self-image after giving birth is also important. Feeling vivacious, strong and beautiful are the benefits of a good walking and exercise program before, during and after pregnancy.*

Anne Kashiwa

It's a good idea to exercise while you're pregnant, and walking allows you to do so in the safest possible way. Fitness walking is particularly good for pregnant women because of its low impact, and because the intensity can be geared to virtually any fitness level.

EFFECTS OF TRAINING

While it was once thought that exercise might increase the chance of miscarriage or stillbirth, there is no scientific evidence to support this belief.

Some research has shown important fitness benefits to the mother from exercising during pregnancy. A study at the University of Wisconsin by Collins and colleagues placed twelve pregnant women in a supervised exercise program at 70 percent of their aerobic capacity. Eight additional women did not participate in the exercise program and served as control subjects. The exercise group had an 18 percent improvement in aerobic capacity, while the control group had a 4 percent decline. A comparison of pregnancy outcome showed no differences between groups in pregnancy duration, labor duration, Apgar scores, birth weight or birth length. This study demonstrates that carefully controlled exercise training during pregnancy is probably not detrimental to the mother or fetus, and may help preserve or even improve fitness level for the mother.

WHO SHOULD EXERCISE?

As the number of women wishing to exercise during pregnancy has grown, the need for more sound medical and scientific advice has also increased. Because of the difficulty of doing research on the effects of exercise during pregnancy, there are few standards and guidelines. Fortunately, there are a few good resources (see references at the end of this chapter).

Clearly, the best time to *improve* your cardiovascular fitness level is before pregnancy. Your fitness walking program during pregnancy should be used to *maintain* fitness levels.

You *can start* an exercise program while pregnant, but this decision should only be made after consultation with your obstetrician. Exercise training is *not* appropriate for every pregnant woman: your obstetrician will consider your medical history and experiences with past pregnancies, and help you develop a safe exercise plan. If you have high blood pressure, anemia, thyroid disease, diabetes or are overweight, your physician may advise that you not exercise or that you modify your exercise, or may recommend a medically supervised program.

EXERCISE GUIDELINES DURING PREGNANCY

Once you and your physician have decided that an exercise program is appropriate for you, choosing the type of aerobic exercise that is safe both to you and the fetus is of primary concern. Obviously, you want to select an activity that you find enjoyable and can perform relatively comfortably. A number of aerobic activities are safe for pregnant women with proper instruction and guidance, including walking, swimming, rowing, cycling, jogging, a combined walk/jog program and cross-country skiing. Activities that involve physical contact or the possibility of excessive jarring or injury to the fetus obviously should be avoided. It is *strongly advised that you become involved in a supervised exercise program where both mother and fetus can be carefully and regularly monitored*. It's also important to maintain communication with your obstetrician throughout your pregnancy, reporting any warning signs (listed later in this chapter) or problems you feel might be associated with your exercise program.

EXERCISE PRESCRIPTION

The exercise prescription for pregnant women is based on the same three basic principles as discussed in Chapter 7: frequency, intensity and duration. They must be modified, however, owing to the physical, hormonal and emotional changes that occur during pregnancy. Exercising beyond the stated guidelines can be dangerous and detrimental both to you and your fetus, so it is crucial that you follow the exercise prescription to the letter. If you're not exercising in a supervised program, always err on the side of caution. Overdoing it can result in extreme increases in body temperature and decreased blood flow to the uterus. Both of these conditions are potentially harmful to the fetus. For this same reason, you should take care not to become dehydrated while walking.

Your exact exercise prescription will be determined by your physical activity and fitness level prior to pregnancy and your exercise goals. Taking the Rockport Fitness Walking Test will help you determine a starting point for your program, but the test should not be taken after the first trimester. After this point, or if you have not been involved in a regular aerobic exercise program, start with the LOW LEVEL fitness walking program.

If you weren't involved in a regular aerobic program before pregnancy, exercise a maximum of three sessions per week, and gradually work up to thirty minutes per session. For women with little prior experience with exercise, heart rate will be the only guide for intensity. Start your program at 60 percent of your predicted maximum heart rate (as described in Chapter 2) and work up to 70 percent in eight to ten weeks. Progress gradually to ensure safety and enjoyment, and avoid burn-out. Continue to monitor your heart rate frequently until you become familiar with what it feels like to be exercising at 60 percent to 70 percent of maximum heart rate.

If you were involved in an exercise program before your pregnancy, you should not exercise any harder during pregnancy. An intensity of 70 percent of your maximum predicted heart rate is a safe level. Your perceived exertion—the feelings associated with a particular intensity of exercise—should be no higher during your fitness walks while pregnant than it was during exercise prior to pregnancy. Most likely, this will mean slowing down your walking pace as you gain weight.

A WORD OF CAUTION

Dizziness (outside of positional changes) during any active portion of your walking program can indicate problems or complications. *Dizziness is not a normal response to exercise and should be reported to your obstetrician as soon as possible.* Becoming dizzy or symptomatic during walking is not a common occurrence during pregnancy but it *can* happen, and you should be aware of the ways to alleviate the dizziness, especially if you should find yourself alone. If you become dizzy, *immediately stop* whatever you are doing and sit down. If you find that sitting does not relieve the dizziness, or you are feeling worse, lie down on your left side with your left arm positioned so that your head can rest on it. Remain in that position until the dizzy feelings have subsided and then use the technique described later in this chapter to sit up. Do not stand up if you are still dizzy. Obviously, if this were ever to happen to you, judging how you feel and using common sense would be the most important guideline. Because these rare, but real, problems can develop, walk in a well-traveled area in case you need some assistance. *Walking alone in remote areas is not advised.*

WARM-UP

Warming up is particularly important, but there are some adjustments to the normal routine that should be made. During pregnancy, joints soften and become less stable, so it is important to avoid stretching to the point of maximum resistance. The warm-up phase should consist of five minutes of a gradual increase in heart rate by slow walking followed by five to ten minutes of slow, gradual stretching. The added weight of the fetus and the resultant change in the center of gravity can throw off your balance and make certain stretches difficult. Most pregnant women find it more comfortable and efficient to perform their stretches while sitting on the floor. Most exercises can be adapted to this position with a little bit of thought about which muscles or muscle groups need to be stretched. Remember to stretch the major muscle groups you will be using during the aerobic phase of your program—the front and backs of your thighs, your calves and your torso.

Late in your pregnancy, you may find yourself in an awkward position, wondering how in the world you're going to get out of it. If after you finish stretching you find yourself lying flat on your back and facing just this problem, roll onto your left side and use both arms to push yourself up to a sitting position. This technique will enable a smooth transition from one position to another. To avoid dizziness or loss of balance, don't rise or change positions too quickly.

SPECIAL TONING/STRENGTHENING EXERCISES

Due to the change in the center of gravity and the growth of the fetus, there is increased physical stress on the muscles and skeleton of the lower back and abdomen. Regular exercises can strengthen the muscles that support the skeleton in these parts of your body. Another important area to strengthen is the pelvic floor. These muscles aid in the delivery of the baby. Many good abdominal/lower back and pelvic floor exercises can be found in chapters 2 and 3 of *Essential Exercises for the Childbearing Years* by Elizabeth Noble (see references at the end of this chapter). Following are a few recommended exercises.

1. *Pelvic tilt:* The pelvic tilt is an exercise that strengthens abdominal muscles while relaxing the back muscles, thus helping to relieve lower back pain. Lie on your back with your knees bent. Roll the pelvis back by contracting your abdominal muscles and flattening your lower back down on the floor. Hold this position for five to ten seconds and then relax; do not hold your breath during the exercise. Repeat three times.
2. *Modified sit-up:* Lie on your back with your knees bent and arms either folded across your chest or held outstretched. Curl your head and shoulders up to about a 45 degree angle, or about eight inches off the floor. Slowly return to the floor. You should breathe out as you curl and breathe in as you return to the starting position.
3. *Diagonal sit-up:* This is a modification of the sit-up designed to strengthen the abdominal muscles toward your sides. As you curl up, reach forward with your outstretched arms to the outside of the left knee. Slowly return to the starting position and then repeat the movement to the right.

Pelvic tilt. *Photo: David Brownell*

Modified sit-up. *Photo: David Brownell*

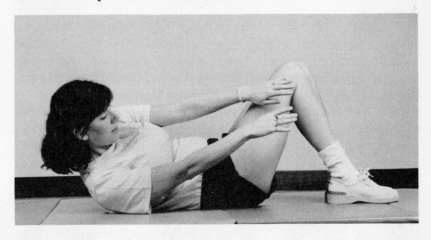

Diagonal sit-up. *Photo: David Brownell*

COOL-DOWN

Always last, but never least, of course, is the cool-down, and it's as important for the pregnant woman as it is for all exercisers. For an explanation and specific recommendations of the cool-down phase, see Chapter 2.

WARNING SIGNS AND SYMPTOMS

If you have any of the following signs or symptoms during your walking program or through the course of your pregnancy, you should stop your exercise program and contact your physician:

1. pain
2. vaginal bleeding
3. dizziness/faintness
4. shortness of breath (not characteristic of your exercise)
5. irregular heart beats or exceptionally fast heart rate
6. absence of fetal movement
7. excessive back pain
8. pubic pain
9. difficulty walking

PRECAUTIONS AND SPECIAL CONSIDERATIONS

TEMPERATURE: • To avoid excessive body temperatures and thus excessive fetal temperature, carefully follow your exercise guidelines. Walk at a moderate intensity and pace and never exercise when you have a fever or on very hot and humid days. See the guidelines for exercising in the heat in Chapter 2.
ROUND LIGAMENT PAIN: • Round ligaments are supportive ligaments located on either side of the uterus, which are composed of muscle tissue, blood vessels and nerves. Their role is to stabilize the uterus during pregnancy and minimize forward-backward and side-to-side motion. Certain activities, especially weight-bearing ones like brisk walking, may cause your uterus to move within the abdominal cavity and pull on the round ligaments, creating a "tugging" or "pulling" sensation. It is

also sometimes described as a "side stitch" or "side ache."

The following five strategies were developed by the Exercising for Two program at Madison General Hospital in Madison, Wisconsin, to relieve round ligament pain.

1. Minimizing the abruptness of your movements may prevent round ligament discomfort. Gradually ease into your exercise pace by walking slowly for about five minutes.
2. Bending forward slowly sometimes quickly relieves the tension on the ligament, and you may then be able to continue with your activity.
3. Some people have found relief by using their hand to support the abdominal wall on the side opposite the "pull."
4. Maintaining abdominal tone by, for instance, maintaining a pelvic tilted position while walking provides support for the uterus and minimizes round ligament discomfort.
5. If all else fails, switch to an alternative activity. For example, switch from walking to stationary cycling or rowing.

FITNESS WALKING AS A PART OF AN OVERALL PROGRAM FOR A HEALTHY PREGNANCY

This book has emphasized the fact that fitness walking should be combined with other positive lifestyle choices to promote health. This is particularly true during pregnancy. In addition to regular exercise, you need to pay particular attention to diet, weight gain and other daily habits during pregnancy.

During pregnancy your requirements for total calories, protein, calcium and iron all increase. Check with your obstetrician or dietician for specific guidance. Your weight should be monitored on a weekly basis. Recent scientific studies have shown that alcohol consumption and cigarette smoking may have serious adverse effects on your baby, and both should be avoided during pregnancy.

FITNESS WALKING AFTER BABY

Fitness walking remains an excellent exercise after childbirth. You can resume fitness walking following delivery, as soon as

Anne introduces her son, Hennie, to the joys of fitness walking.
Photo: Ernie Leyba

your body tells you it's ready. With normal vaginal delivery, you can begin gentle walking as soon as it causes no pain. This will typically be within a few days after delivery; however, if you had an episiotomy or Caesarean section, the recovery period will be longer. See Chapter 10, "Walking for Rehabilitation," for more on returning to normal activity.

Once your strength returns, start taking your baby with you, preferably in a pack-type carrier. Recent research, reported in the British medical journal *The Lancet*, suggests that babies who are regularly carried on their mother's body during their first year of life may be calmer and cry less. The study also suggested that these babies were more secure and independent, dealing better with separation from Mom and contact with strangers.

One last word of encouragement to new mothers. Gone are the days when motherhood brought an end to athletic participation. Today's women athletes, including runners Mary Decker Slaney and Valerie Brisco-Hooks and racewalker Maryanne Torellas, have demonstrated this stunningly. Torellas returned to competition in 1987 after the birth of her third child and won the Indoor National Racewalking Championship, setting a new American record for the 5K in the process.

Said one athlete and mother, "I think God gives mothers extra endurance, because he knows they'll need it." Whatever the reason, it's clear that Moms can lace up their shoes and perform with the best of 'em.

FURTHER READING

A few references are now available in the general area of exercise during pregnancy. Some that we can recommend are:

- American College of Obstetricians and Gynecologists. Exercise During Pregnancy and the Post-natal Period. Washington, D.C.: American College of Obstetricians and Gynecologists, 1985. (Available through your obstetrician.)
- Artal, Raul, and Wiswell, Robert, eds. *Exercise in Pregnancy: Experimental and Clinical Management*. Baltimore: Williams and Wilkins Co., 1985. (This is an academic and research-oriented book containing very technical information.)

- Noble, Elizabeth. *Essential Exercises for the Childbearing Years.* Boston: Houghton Mifflin, 1982. (A good source for special exercise during and after pregnancy.)
- Shangold, Mona, and Mirkin, Gabe. *The Complete Medicine Book for Women.* New York: Simon & Schuster, 1985. (An excellent general reference on exercise and sports for women, with a short but good chapter on pregnancy.)

10
Walking for Rehabilitation

Unfortunately, there are times in your life when you find your-self flat on your back, your body temporarily put out of com-mission by illness, injury or surgery. When you're finally back on your feet, you may find your body is frustratingly weak and out of shape from disuse, or perhaps even completely changed by an operation. During your period of inactivity, a number of physiological and psychological changes have occurred, changes that put you in need of rehabilitation—and walking can be an invaluable part of the process.

In addition, even in a safe sport like walking you can suffer an occasional sports injury from which you need to work your way back to normal activity. Or you may be turning to walking now because you've had an injury, acute or chronic, that makes you unable to participate in another sport. This chapter, com-bined with a little good sense and restraint, can safely guide you back to your desired level of activity.

DECONDITIONING

While this book has focused on what it means to train your body, there is a reverse process, called deconditioning, that results from inactivity and has drastic results. In one Swedish study, five healthy medical students were bed-rested for twenty-one days. Forced to be inactive, their physical condition began to decline, and by the end of three weeks, they had lost 27 percent of their cardiovascular fitness. In addition, their muscles atrophied—became smaller and weaker—owing to disuse. The good news is that given roughly the same amount of time, you can recapture your fitness, but it may be frustrating at first.

Psychologically, many women (and men) who've been laid up have to contend with a feeling of loss of control over their bodies. Feelings of decreased self-esteem and independence can lead to depression, with physical symptoms including sleeplessness, anxiety and constipation. This experience is particularly common after surgery, and most extreme after an operation that results in a change in the body, like a mastectomy.

GETTING BACK ON YOUR FEET

While the illnesses and accidents that knock you out are almost always unexpected, you can do one important piece of planning for recovery: stay in good shape. Without a doubt, if you're in good physical condition you'll recover more quickly from illness or injury. Weight is an obvious component: if you're obese, doctors say, it's like going into surgery with two strikes against you.

Once you know you're going to be laid up, explain to your physician how important exercise is to you, and get specific advice and instruction on returning to normal activity. This is particularly important because a recent study found that less than 10 percent of doctors give any advice about exercise to their patients.

Finally, and most important, give yourself a break. Recognize and accept that your abilities have been limited, and let your body tell you how much it's ready to do. Pain is a crucial stop sign when you're rehabilitating.

RECOVERING FROM SURGERY

After any surgical procedure there are considerable advantages to getting back on your feet quickly. Walking after an operation works to prevent several common, but serious, surgical complications: urinary tract infection; venous thrombosis—blood clots in the legs; pulmonary embolism—blood clots that have traveled to the lungs; and ileus—slowing of the bowel that results in painful gas and constipation.

The operations from which you may be recovering can be broken down into five categories: major vaginal, minor vaginal, abdominal wall, orthopedic, and mastectomy. (Cardiovascular rehabilitation will be dealt with separately later in the chapter.)

1. *Major vaginal surgery* includes a vaginal delivery, or a vaginal hysterectomy in which the abdominal wall is not cut. There may be sutures and soreness, but as long as there is no incision in the abdomen you can generally be up and exercising mildly in four to five days.
2. *Minor vaginal surgery*, generally a dilatation and curettage (D and C); while you may be sore, you can probably walk the next day.
3. *Abdominal wall*, including gall bladder surgery, Caesarean section and stomach surgery, limits walking greatly, because the abdominal muscles are involved in lifting the legs. In the ten days following surgery, don't disrupt the scar formation; thereafter, use common sense. Any pain should be reported to your physician. If you were active before your surgery, you can slowly walk your way back to your usual vigor. However, while you may be able to return to normal activities after a month, you'll need to be patient: it may be up to six months before you feel like your old self, physically.
4. *Orthopedic*, particularly leg and back surgery, varies widely depending on the extent and nature of the operation. In general, though, there is a need to protect the recovering body part while maintaining a degree of cardiovascular fitness and combating disuse atrophy and decreased range of motion. First, you can do simple range-of-motion exercises, perhaps even while you are still in bed. The second stage of recovery is nonweight-bearing activity, like a stationary

---

Despite recent interest in exercise, the U.S. Public Health Service estimates that only 20 percent of the adult population get enough exercise for substantial improvement in cardiovascular health.

bike for cardiovascular conditioning. Finally, you'll be ready for controlled weight-bearing exercise, like walking.

5. *Breast cancer:* Following a radical mastectomy, jarring activity, like walking, can be painful. There are early reaching exercises that can be done with the affected arm to speed recovery. The American Cancer Society offers an excellent pamphlet on the subject. Later, the walking arm swing can be used as a gentle movement to strengthen the arm.

Often more important in these cases is the psychological impact of the surgery. Feelings of violation and a damaged self-image are enormous blows from which to recover. While there are a number of important factors that can help a woman through this difficult experience, walking can be a valuable reassertion of independence and physical well being.

RECOVERING FROM INJURY

In this case, there are two types of injury from which walking can help you recover: acute and chronic.

1) ACUTE INJURIES. · While walking is a particularly safe physical activity, it's good to be aware of a few pitfalls. Always let pain be your indicator: soreness—a generalized achey feeling—doesn't usually indicate an injury. Localized pain of sudden onset or soreness that lasts longer than forty-eight hours *does*, and should be examined by a doctor.

If you misstep and feel a sharp pain in your knee or ankle, particularly if accompanied by a popping sound, you may have a sprain. Sprains, graded in severity from first degree (mild) to third degree (severe), are the stretching and tearing of ligaments—the fibrous tissue that connects one bone to another. Treatment of a sprain should be immediate, to minimize swelling. Don't keep walking, and *don't* put heat on the affected joint. The key to recovery is RICE: *rest*—get off the injured joint; *ice*, which should be applied repeatedly—twenty minutes on, thirty minutes off; *compression*—wrap the injured joint in an Ace cotton elastic bandage; and *elevation*—get off your feet and prop the injured ankle on a chair.

If the joint won't support your weight after the accident, or if pain is severe, seek medical attention. If swelling is minor, and the pain subsides quickly, the best treatment is rest, ice and an antiinflammatory (two aspirin every four hours). You should start walking again as soon as you can do it without pain. You may need to start out slowly and see how much activity your recovering joint will bear.

New sports medicine techniques, originally developed to speed top athletes back to competition, are now available to any active woman. Treatment at a sports medicine center can help you recover quickly, and minimize the risk of recurrence. Even after a relatively severe sprain, it's possible to be back to par in fewer than two months.

2) *CHRONIC INJURIES.* • Also known as overuse injuries, chronic injuries include a variety of knee ailments, tendinitis, shin splints and stress fractures. The best strategy here is avoidance: proper warm-up and cool-down, use of proper shoes and good sense all fight chronic injury. Attempting to walk a good deal farther, or faster, than you normally do is an invitation to this sort of problem.

If you experience lingering soreness in one spot of your body, try the R-I portion of the above prescription: rest and ice. Aspirin may help, too. Beyond that, you may have to examine your mechanics—your stride or your foot motion. Even if your pain is in your knee or your hip, you may need to see an orthopedist or podiatrist about placing orthotics in your shoes to correct a biomechanical problem.

RECOVERING FROM SEVERE ILLNESS

There are so many possibilities within this category that there can be no general guidelines. Expect a degree of deconditioning; alert your physician to your desire to be active, and be patient as you work yourself back to your previous condition.

CARDIAC REHABILITATION

Much of the early interest in walking came from the experience of hundreds of heart patients who participated in walking pro-

FITNESS WALKING FOR CARDIAC REHABILITATION
PHASE II: Fitness Walking Immediately Following Hospital Discharge*

Week	Warm-up	Pace (mph)	Heart Rate	Duration (mins.)	Cool-down	Frequency (times per week)	Other
1	10–15 mins. before-walk stretches†	1.5	RHR +10‡	15	15 mins. after-walk stretches†	5	education/ risk factor reduction§
2	"	2.0	"	20	"	"	"
3	"	2.0	"	30	"	"	"
4	"	2.0	RHR +15	40	"	"	"
5	"	2.0	"	50	"	"	"
6	"	2.0	"	60	"	"	"
7	"	2.5	RHR +15	40	"	"	"
8**	"	2.5	"	45	"	"	"
9	"	2.5	"	50	"	"	"
10	"	2.5	"	60	"	"	"

*Fitness walking for cardiac rehabilitation should not be undertaken without the consent of your personal physician.

†See pages 29–44 for recommended sequence of before- and after-walking stretches.

‡RHR means "resting heart rate." Measure your heart rate at rest, then exercise at the prescribed heart rate as indicated. (See page 45 for the proper technique of pulse taking.)

§Education about heart disease and risk factor reduction are important components of cardiac rehabilitation. (See page 17.)

**At Week 8 we recommend an exercise test on a treadmill supervised by your physician.

grams as part of their rehabilitation at the U/Mass Medical Center. Patients loved their walking programs—they helped restore confidence, and actively involved the patient in recovery. As one woman stated, "After my heart attack, my walking program helped me to take charge of my life and develop new, better habits."

Walking isn't the only component of cardiac rehabilitation for patients who have suffered a heart attack, have angina or have undergone coronary artery bypass surgery or angioplasty. But a walking program serves as the cornerstone of virtually every cardiac rehabilitation program in the world.

A walking program to use as a part of an overall cardiac rehabilitation program is found at the end of this chapter. Rather than using a target heart rate, it indicates number of heart beats above resting heart rate, starting with an increase of 10. Remember, cardiac rehabilitation is serious business—don't try to do it alone. It is very important that your program be carried out under the supervision of a qualified physician.

Another area of concern is Beta blockers, drugs that slow an individual's heart rate and lower blood pressure, and are commonly prescribed for individuals who have angina. While you can still enjoy most of the physical and psychological benefits of walking, the area of improved cardiovascular fitness while on Beta blockers remains somewhat controversial. At this point, the weight of evidence suggests that some beneficial changes do occur. If you are on a Beta blocker medication, you should get specific recommendations from your physician before starting a fitness walking program.

In the United States, about 50 percent of all women have had hysterectomies by the age of 65.

A member of the Mexican women's racewalking team demonstrates excellent form. *Photo: Paul Potera*

11
Racewalking

May 11, 1986. This was it. This was the day for which I had been training and sweating for over two months. The Rockport Grand Walk Series had come to town.

The challenge came to me two months earlier when I witnessed the Grand Walk 10K racewalk on a clear, cold morning in Washington, D.C. The race course was one of the most beautiful I had ever seen—running between the Lincoln Memorial and the Vietnam Memorial, it took the walkers around the Reflecting Pond several times.

As a spectator that brisk morning, I was wondering if the racers' adrenaline was keeping them warmer than I felt. As they gathered at the starting line, I wasn't sure if the trembling I saw was from cold or nerves, but the excitement in the air was infectious.

The gun sounded and all I could think of was how much I wanted to be out there with them. Like all great athletes, they made their sport look so easy, and I thought to myself "I can do that!" Considering myself to be a decent athlete, and having previously participated in several running races, I thought I could racewalk if I trained for it.

The sight of those women so inspired me that when I returned home to Colorado I immediately started training for the May race scheduled in Denver.

I quickly found that training was not going to be as easy as I had anticipated, but I didn't get discouraged. The picture in my memory of those graceful yet powerful women in full stride, their images reflected in the water, was hard to erase. For the first two weeks I was sore from the top of my head to the tip of my toes. I could barely get out of bed in the morning.

The third week was much smoother and more satisfying; my technique and pace began to feel right. I started training for speed, and since I lived at eight thousand feet in the foothills of the Rockies, I added a little hill training.

The next thirty days were rewarding as well as disappointing. There were times when I had to ask myself why I was doing this. But having a definite goal helped keep me going.

Almost before I knew it, it seemed, I was at Washington Park in Denver, getting warmed up in the company of the same women I had admired two months before. I discovered that the trembling—at least mine—was not from the cold, since it was a warm, beautiful morning, and I was shaking all over. After a pep talk from my husband and one-year-old son, I stepped up to the starting line. I was feeling pretty confident—I really had put my heart and soul into this—but it was still hard not to be intimidated by the nationally ranked athletes.

Well, the rest is history. I raced and was very pleased with myself, until Teresa Vaill lapped me with a mile to go. I tried not to be discouraged; after all, this was a champion that just passed me. But, oh how hard it was to see her go by . . .

I stopped the clock at just a little over an hour and three minutes. Teresa had finished in 58:24. I was in awe, but I was also very proud of myself for finishing and posting a respectable time. I have since had better races, but I will never forget the excitement and experience I got that very first time.

Anne Kashiwa

Olympic and World-class racewalkers like Teresa are the ultimate fitness walkers. This elite group of women and men are leaders in the sport of racewalking, which is slowly reaching a growing number of enthusiasts through events like the Grand Walk Series.

Exercise physiologists have found World-class racewalkers to have a level of cardiovascular fitness comparable to that of marathon runners. In addition, their body fat percentages were found to be very low; again, comparable to elite endurance athletes in sports such as running, cycling and rowing. Clearly, the demands of racewalking are every bit as strenuous as performance in any other endurance activity. As the popularity of this activity grows, the public will slowly come to understand the high level of endurance and skill possessed by top race-walkers.

The racewalker's exacting technique—the exaggerated body movement, the forward thrust of the hip, the pumping arms and rolling gait—evoke amusement among most first-time spectators. Even *The Wall Street Journal* refers to racewalkers as ". . . the Rodney Dangerfields of the sports world—they don't get no respect." Only when it is apparent that a champion racewalker has completed a mile in seven minutes or so does the laughter subside and admiration, even amazement, set in.

America's top women consistently post winning times of twenty-three to twenty-four minutes in the 5K races. To put this in perspective, this means walking at an average pace of seven minutes and thirty seconds per mile throughout the 3.1 mile race. It is a bit disturbing to note, however, that race-walking is an Olympic sport only for men. As history has shown, however, it should only be a matter of time before women as well can compete in Olympic stadiums.

TECHNIQUE

To better understand the sport of racewalking, it is important to grasp the fundamental techniques, the differences in style that distinguish competitive racewalking from its distant cousin, fitness walking.

Racewalking involves adaptation of ordinary walking techniques for competitive purposes. It enables you to take longer strides with higher frequency, which results in faster walking.

According to the rulebook of the Amateur Athletic Federation, racewalking is defined as a progression of steps so taken that unbroken contact with the ground is maintained. Also, the supporting leg must be straight at the knee when in the vertical,

There was no officially sanctioned racewalking competition for women until 1979, when a 10K (6.2-mile) race was established by the International Amateur Athletic Federation.

upright position. The distinction here is simple: once the knee is bent, the stride becomes running.

Technique may seem overwhelming at first, but that's part of the challenge of any sport. Take the learning process one step at a time and be patient in looking for results; and, as with any other sport, don't overtrain—excessive mileage can put even the best of athletes on the sidelines.

What you're striving for is a rhythmic, flowing movement. By developing the upper and lower body evenly, the racewalker develops supple balance and coordination. Basically, it works like this: the heel-to-toe action provides forward momentum; the legs work against the resistance of the ground to propel the body foward; the hips rotate to increase stride length, and the shortened arm swing adds balance and drive. Let's slow it down and look at it part by part:

TRUNK POSITION. • Forward lean should come from the ankles, and not from bending at the waist. Imagine a ski jumper in the air; all the lean is from the ankles and the upper body is straight. Obviously, walkers will not lean to such extremes, but it is the same idea.

STRIDE. • Walkers who are new to the sport are advised to develop a comfortable stride that is appropriate for their size. As your technique improves your stride will automatically become longer.

ARM SWING. • Racewalking utilizes more muscle groups than fitness walking because of the vigorous use of the upper body and arms. The arm swing is not a forced movement but the natural front-to-back motion of the arms, bent at a 90-degree angle at the elbow for forward thrust and increased momentum. If the elbow is bent too much it shortens your stride and may pull the body upward, causing the foot to lose contact with the ground. If the elbow is not bent enough, however, the arm movements may be too long, thus losing the economy of the whole movement. The hands should not swing above midchest or more than six inches behind your hips. They should also

---

Racewalking exerts pressure of only one and a quarter times the body's weight on the joints, whereas running exerts three to four times the body's weight.

remain above hip level, and shouldn't cross the imaginary line dividing the right and left sides of your body.

HIP MOTION • Anyone who has witnessed an elite racewalking event is aware of the exaggerated hip movement necessary to achieve the quick gliding stride. If your hip can move freely front-to-back, it can increase your stride length up to 25 percent. The hips also go up and down in a rolling motion. This smooths out your pace, which would otherwise become jerky because of the straightening of the leg.

FOOT POSITION. • Pointing your feet forward, with no outward deviation, will give you longer steps and a more powerful impulse. Your heel should contact the ground clearly ahead of your body at the beginning of each step, and your feet should land directly in front of each other. To practice this, walking on a straight line is good exercise.

FURTHER RESOURCES

For more information (and a directory of local racewalking clubs), send a self-addressed stamped envelope to Sal Corallo, Racewalking Chairman, The Athletes Congress, P.O. Box 120, Indianapolis, IN 46206. Also, check the competition pages of *The Walking Magazine*. A national organization was founded recently called The North American Racewalking Foundation (NARF); write to them at P.O. Box 50312, Pasadena, CA 91109.

If you think you might like to enter a race, an expanding schedule of competitive events is helping to spread interest in the sport and provide experience for novice or intermediate racewalkers. The competition is always friendly and helpful. If you decide to compete, here are four basic tips.

1. Warm-up is crucial. The upper body, including shoulders, arms and trunk, should be limber, since tightness can make for a slower and unpleasant race. A warm-up walk before the race is a necessity to loosen buttocks, legs and feet.
2. Concentrate on one aspect of technique at a time, and be patient with your progress. Don't forget to breathe normally while on the course.
3. Prior to any race, make sure you have had ample training

time and are familiar with the distance you are going to walk. On race day, get to the site early to check in, warm up and, yes, take that nervous body to the restroom.

4. Finally, find your place at the starting line. If you are the aggressive type, go to the front of the pack. If you feel more comfortable in the back, that's fine, too. Pat yourself on the back for being there and when the starting gun sounds, wish yourself luck and have a great race.

If competing doesn't appeal to you, don't pass up the excellent conditioning benefits of racewalking. Once you attain a fitness walking pace of twelve-minute miles, stepping up to racewalking is an excellent way to give yourself a new challenge and continue to improve your fitness level.

> Racewalking has been an Olympic event for men since 1908.

12
Adventure Walking

As fitness walking has become more popular among women, a few individuals have been active in pushing back the boundaries of what had previously been regarded as limits for women in sports. We are very pleased that our friend and colleague Jan Reynolds, who has participated in numerous treks throughout the world, agreed to contribute the following chapter on adventure walking. In this chapter, Jan describes some of her incredible experiences, as well as providing some specific tips to help you if you should decide to go on an adventure of your own.

I am alone, feeling inconsequential, almost intimidated, by the sheer magnitude of the expanse around my fragile tent whipping in the up-valley winds. The sharp, cracking sounds of the shifting glacial ice and the loud turbulence of the avalanches echo up the moraine floor and bounce off the high peaks. The moody skies have been darkening and are spitting snow into the winds. It's the twenty-fifth of May, and the mountain weather still hasn't cleared. Being ill with this nasty virus while camped here at seventeen thousand five hundred feet has made me too weak to cross the moraine and travel the two or three days down-valley to get provisions, so I haven't eaten for a few days, and my last supply of tea is all but gone. The snow is beginning to mount up around the thin nylon which separates me from the outside. I feel too tired to feel too concerned.

As I reread my journals I remember I felt comforted rather than frightened when I heard sounds, then voices, before four eyes peered into my tent through a slit unzipped for ventilation. Two small Sherpas began speaking shyly but quickly. I understood a little, but our sign language conveyed the most com-

Jan Reynolds climbing Mount Pumori during the first winter ascent
by Americans of the Himalayas during the Everest Grand Circle
Expedition. In the background looms Mount Everest. *Photo: Ned
Gillette*

munication. They were asking for something to cover themselves
from the snow and howling winds for the night. Instead, I
invited or, rather, encouraged them into my tent for the night
to dispel the harsh chill. The men were Passang and his son,
Tsa Wong. When they saw that I was not well and had nothing
to eat they started a fire with the yak dung they had collected
and brewed up a strong batch of Tibetan tea—a thick mixture
of dark tea leaves, yak butter, and salt—and made me drink it
to improve my strength. After I drank their tea, Passang encouraged, "Eat tsampa high. Good, strong," in broken English.
Tsampa, or ground barley, and tea became my regular diet.
From that night on I was accepted by these two Sherpas as one
of them and, therefore, was given a chance to become a "local"
in the eyes of all others I met along this fifty-mile ancient salt
trade route stretching from Namcha Barwa, the cultural center
of Nepal's Khumbu, to the town of Tingri on Tibet's dry, wind-
swept fifteen-thousand-foot plateau.

Passang's three yaks had died on this route returning from

Jan crossing the Rakai River in New Zealand during the Southern Cross Expedition. This expedition, which took place in 1979, was the first transverse of the heart of New Zealand on cross-country skis. *Photo: Ned Gillette*

Tibet in early winter when traveling over the Nangpa La, a nineteen-thousand-foot glaciated depression in the Himalayan chain on the Nepal-Tibet border. He was forced to bury his loads of salt in the snow for retrieval this spring. He and Tsa Wong had just been up to the height of the pass and were each lugging down over fifty kilos of salt into Nepal on their backs in handwoven yak hair bags. They were happy to have found me and my shelter to weather out the storm and rest. I was happy to have been found. I had been traveling the trade route myself, with a load of grain, headed for Tibet, covering the story of the ancient exchange of Tibetan salt for Nepalese grain across the high Himalayan peaks for *National Geographic Magazine*.

Days later, when my strength returned, I crossed over the Nangpa La and into Tibet carrying my load of grain and provisions. At the height of the pass I felt small and lonely. I worked my way over and around the crevasse-ridden glacier while buffeted by gelid winds gusting up to forty miles an hour, amidst towering rock and snow faces of the peaks walling in the pass.

When I looked north the Tibetan plateau seemed to stretch out and away forever in soft brown and violet hues, muted and blending together like a watercolor painting. I walked the thirty miles into Tingri in a day and a half to trade my grain, because once off the glacier and rugged rock moraine the terrain was dry and flat. I met a Tibetan trader returning home named Dawa, and we traveled together, gesturing to each other to communicate. When we reached his home in Tingri, I decided to trade my small amount of grain with Dawa, who had become not only my traveling companion, but my teacher and friend. His wife, Mingma, served us tsampa at the hearth of the open fire in the mud-bricked, whitewashed home. Dawa held my hand securely in his two rough hands and grinned after he set a small hand-turned tea bowl in front of me to offer in trade. I blinked back the tears, perhaps because of the memories of everything I'd been through for this one small moment of exchange, or because for the first time I felt the brotherhood of barter myself.

To me, walking over the border from Nepal into Tibet across the Himalayas on the oldest trade route still in use today, via a nineteen-thousand-foot pass used exclusively by the indigenous people, was a true adventure. I see adventure as stepping into the unknown, as unpredictable, something that cannot be calculated or planned. But, because you are walking into unfamiliar territory, an adventure may also entail a certain amount of "sticking your neck out," and blind commitment. Consequently there are risks, but the rewards from an experience of this nature can be great. You are living life to the fullest, challenging your wits, and sometimes warming your heart with unbounded human kindness. For me the risks are worth these rewards. And quite frankly the danger isn't the draw, it's a strong curiosity that compels me. My adventures have taken me around the world several times, from the highest peaks to the largest desert on earth. Some of these travels have demanded honed physical skills, when I have set World climbing and skiing records. Other trips have demanded my writing and photographic skills. But 75 to 90 percent of each adventure was purely walking—my feet taking me where I wanted to go.

Anyone can travel on an adventure walk today. And being a woman is not a limiting factor to setting off on an adventure. Never once in my travels had I wished that I were a man. I have often found it to my advantage to be a female adventurer. For example, I feel my foreign friends have accepted me more readily, perhaps finding me less threatening than my male counterpart. Because I usually travel alone the men respect me on their level, because I share their experience. Yet, I also can slip into the lifestyle of their women at home—thus being able to communicate with both sexes.

But, more important, an adventure doesn't necessarily require the strength or skills to scale peaks or cross glaciers. As always, specificity is the key. To prepare for a long trek merely begin walking at home before you travel. The Rockport Fitness Walking Program is an excellent place to start. If you have the time, don't hesitate to increase your mileage and your pace as you become more fit. The background of an international athlete isn't necessary to set off on an adventure, because your personal adventure zone is merely what is unknown and foreign to you alone. Quite simply adventure walking can be as straightforward as walking through a new neighborhood or over the Golden Gate Bridge.

If you *are* looking for adventure in foreign lands, it isn't necessary to be an expert in international travel. There are several excellent trekking companies willing to plan and guide your travel to both poles and anything that lies in between, be it desert, jungle or mountains.

In 1985, three Australians, two Brits and I set the high altitude record for Alpine flying in hot-air balloons. We flew up to 27,000 feet in hopes of flying over the world's highest peak, 29,028-foot Mount Everest. Although we flew higher than any other balloonists in mountainous terrain and floated as if in a dream over some of the world's most spectacular geography, we missed our mark. I watched one of our two balloons fall out of the sky for 11,000 feet before relighting the failed pilot lights. Our balloon, like the other, ran short on gas and was forced to crash land on a cliff side.

In order to prepare for the World record flight our crew trekked into the mountains to test equipment. Because we were extremely busy with flight preparations, our entire trek into the Himalayas was organized for us by a large, international trekking organization. We traveled with the local Sherpas, who set up and broke camp for us every day, cooked our meals and carried our loads. They even woke us in the morning by offering us sweet, warm tea, while we were still snuggled in our sleeping bags. On this trek we were free to work with our balloon gear, record the weather, photograph and simply enjoy ourselves. This was a luxury to which I was not accustomed, but highly recommend. A travel agent can put you in touch with some of the large trekking organizations, such as Mountain Travel or Sobek, but don't stop there. Many small operations and independent guides will arrange specific treks at the client's request. Look in the back pages of *The Walking Magazine* or of many outdoor and climbing and skiing magazines, such as *Outside, Backpacker* or *Powder* for these offerings. Or, best of all, talk to someone who has already been on an adventure travel trip. The main thing before signing up or hiring a guide is to determine whether you would like to meet new, interesting people on a preorganized trek or travel only with acquaintances in a specific area of your choice.

If you are high spirited and independent you can certainly arrange for your adventure walk on your own. When I traveled to Morocco in the winter of 1985 to ski off Mt. Toubkal, the country's highest peak of almost fourteen thousand feet in the High Atlas, I organized the adventure never having been there before. I called the World Health Organization to find out what shots I might need. I contacted the Moroccan Embassy in Washington, D.C., to find out what type of permits or visas I might need. I called my travel agent at least a month ahead of departure time to begin bargain shopping for plane tickets and was given the same health and visa information by the agency as well. A good travel agency can often give you all the information you will need for preparation. I bought several books on Morocco and began poring over maps. I read about and located huts in the High Atlas. Travel guides gave me an idea of temperature and weather, so I knew what to bring for clothing. I always pack light and prepare myself to be self-sufficient if I need to, by bringing a sleeping bag, bivouac sack, small campstove and a medical kit. My med kit contains mainly a pain killer and antibiotics, but also medicines for colds, aspirin, etc. Other valuable items to take along are a headlamp or flashlight; a daypack for personal items if your gear is being portered or carried by a pack animal; and, of course, sturdy, durable shoes with good support. For more rugged terrain or cold temperatures I use a light hiking boot with a patterned sole and wear heavy wool socks.

With the help of local people, public transportation, guide books and my broken French, my friend Bad and I managed to get to the hut at the base of Toubkal with the provisions we would need to ski the peak. I arranged for a donkey and driver to carry our gear to the snow line. I often find locals will porter loads or hire out their animals for a fair price. We used our map and legs to get ourselves to another hut four thousand feet below the height of the peak. Many countries have hut systems open to the public to facilitate your adventure, but don't let the lack of huts deter you; a tent can do just as well.

We were up at the crack of dawn to climb to the summit after a beautiful dump of dry powder snow from a storm that had traveled in over the Sahara. We laughed and giggled as we skied down the four thousand vertical feet, intertwining our tracks to make a long ribbon of figure eights over a cascading stairway of snow. Some Italian Alpinists had just arrived when we reached the bottom of the last pitch and were surprised to see that we had descended the challenging slope with style on cross-country skis.

While traveling I offered currency for arranged rides, rather than hitchhiking, and wore a small fanny pack or wallet hung around my neck to carry my passport and travelers checks or any other valuables for safekeeping. I am friendly but cautious when in foreign countries. Our ski descent of Toubkal went on to be published in ski magazines, after we skied the dunes of the Sahara as well. It was a fun adventure, largely because it was thought out thoroughly and well organized, but executed with a flexible plan.

My best allies on my adventures have been my Walkman personal stereo, good books and a miniature portable chessboard. Four of us spent one week stormed in by a raging blizzard in a two-man tent in the New Zealand Alps in 1979. The chessboard became key to our existence and fed our minds, while our bodies lay prone, packed like sardines. We walked out of the mountains in only two days once the storm subsided.

The claustrophobia of being pinned down for a week in a tent or snow cave in a storm in New Zealand, like the pain of skiing at high altitude, the physical strain and discomfort while circling Mount Everest and the extreme danger involved in ballooning over the Himalayas, was forgotten soon after the event, and the treasured moments remain in my mind.

I think we all can benefit from stepping into our self-determined adventure zones by giving ourselves a chance to experience something unplanned. Walking out on an adventure feeds the spirit of something very basic inside me. Today's predictable patterns and nine-to-five lives call for something to test our reactions and boil our blood to make us feel alive. Maybe we all might feel a little better by lacing up our shoes and walking out on an adventure.

Jan Reynolds

TEN TIPS FOR ADVENTURE WALKING

1. Develop a well-organized, flexible plan.
2. Begin walking for conditioning at home to be in good shape at the start of your trip.

3. Research your destination (weather, elevation, etc.) so you'll be well prepared.
4. Break in your footwear before you go.
5. Use *all* equipment at least once before you go, including tents, rain gear, etc.
6. Take a medical kit, including first aid and antibiotics.
7. Be prepared to be self-sufficient—bring food, stove, shelter, etc.
8. Study your destination. Call the embassy for any necessary permissions or visas. Call the World Health Organization about shots.
9. Befriend locals or hire a tour guide for information and safety.
10. Eat only cooked foods to avoid picking up parasites.

Appendix

Personal Walking Log
  This handy log can be used to chart your mileage as you progress in your twenty-week walking program.

WEEK	DAY 1	DAY 2	DAY 3	DAY 4	DAY 5	DAY 6	DAY 7	WEEKLY TOTAL
1								
2								
3								
4								
5								
6								
7								
8								
9								
10								
11								
12								
13								
14								
15								
16								
17								
18								
19								
20								

References

Book
Sweetgall, Robert, James Rippe, and Frank Katch, with John Dignam. *Fitness Walking*. New York: Perigee Books, 1985.

Pamphlets
Ward, A., and J. Rippe, *Starting Your Personal Fitness Walking Program*, Philadelphia: J. B. Lippincott, 1987.
Ward, A., and J. Rippe. *Walking for Health and Fitness*. Philadelphia: J. B. Lippincott, 1987.

Articles
Rippe, J. M. (Moderator). "Roundtable Discussion: Walking for Fitness." *The Physician and Sportsmedicine* 14: 144.
Porcari, J., R. McCarron, G. Kline, P. Freedson, A. Ward, J. Ross, and J. Rippe. "Is Fast Walking an Adequate Aerobic Training Stimulus in 30 to 69 Year Old Adults?" *The Physician and Sportsmedicine* 15: 119.
Kline, G. M., J. P. Porcari, R. Hintermeister, P. S. Freedson, A. Ward, R. F. McCarron, J. Ross, and J. M. Rippe. "Prediction of VO_2 Max from a One Mile Track Walk." *Med Sci Sports and Exercise* (1987).
Rippe, J. M., A. Ward, and P. S. Freedson. "Walking for Health and Fitness." Encyclopedia Britannica *Health Annual* (1987).

Dr. James Rippe and Anne Kashiwa discuss a chapter outline for *Fitness Walking for Women. Photo: David Brownell*

About the Authors

DR. JAMES RIPPE. • Dr. Rippe is an attending cardiologist and Director of the Exercise Physiology Laboratory at the University of Massachusetts Medical School. He is also the Research Director for the Rockport Walking Institute and Senior Medical Adviser for *The Walking Magazine.* Under Dr. Rippe's leadership the Exercise Physiology Laboratory at U/Mass Medical School has conducted a variety of research projects, published numerous articles and abstracts on various aspects of walking, and presented findings at a number of national medical and scientific conferences. A lifelong and avid athlete, he maintains his physical condition with a daily walk and run program. Dr. Rippe's previous book on walking, co-authored with Robert Sweetgall and Frank Katch, was entitled *Fitness Walking* and was a winner of an American Health Magazine National Book Award in 1985.

ANNE KASHIWA. • Anne Kashiwa is also a lifelong avid athlete who has been involved in a variety of sports including professional racquetball, downhill skiing and running. She is a racewalker who has participated in a number of competitions. She serves as walking consultant for The Rockport Company and as a consultant to fitness and athletic clubs. She is currently the Director of the Oxford Club, an athletic facility located in Denver, Colorado. She lives with her husband, Hank, and son, Hennie, in the foothills of the Rocky Mountains outside of Denver.

Index

A

Abdominal wall, surgery through, 125
Adolescents, fitness walking for, 22
Adventure walking, 137–45
Aerobic exercise, 15–16, 45–46
  weight loss through, 76
Amateur Athletic Federation, 133
American Cancer Society, 126
American College of Sports Medicine, 105
  Guidelines of, 15
American Heart Association (AHA), 61, 80, 81
Anemia, 113
Angina, 16
  medications for, 110, 129
  rehabilitation for, 129
Angioplasty, 129
Ankle circles, 43
Appetite control, 76
Arm swing, 27, 28
  for racewalking,, 134–35

B

Back and leg stretch, 41
Backpacker magazine, 142
Backpacks, weighted, 105
Beta blockers, 110, 129
Body fat measurement, 74
Body weights, walking with, 104–5
Bone strength, 14
Boredom, techniques for battling, 47
Breast cancer, 73
  estrogen therapy and risk of, 90
  rehabilitation after surgery for, 126

Brisco-Hooks, Valerie, 121
Bypass surgery, 129

C

Caesarean section, 125
Calcium, 21, 89–94
Calf stretch, 42
Caloric expenditure, increase in, 76
Cancer, 73
  diet and, 79, 81
Cardiac health benefits, 16–17
Cardiac rehabilitation, 127–29
Cardiac risk factors, 17–18
  diet and, 79, 81
  obesity and, 73
Catecholamines, 20
Childbirth, recovery after, 125
Children, fitness walking for, 22
Cholesterol, 17, 18
  fat and, 81
  fiber and, 86
  limiting intake of, 85
  obesity and, 73
Cigarette smoking, 17
  quitting, 18–19, 25
Clubs, walking, 47, 109
Collins (researcher), 112
Cool-down, 46
  and avoidance of injury, 127
  for pregnant women, 118
  after weight training, 103
Cool weather precautions, 54–55
Corallo, Sal, 135
Coronary artery disease, 16, 17

D

Deconditioning, 123–24, 127
Degenerative joint disease, 73
Deltoid stretch, 38

Diabetes, 14
  as coronary risk factor, 17
  diet and, 79, 81
  obesity and, 73
  during pregnancy, 113
Diagonal sit-up, 116, 117
Diet:
  weight-loss, 75, 78
  See also Nutrition
Dilatation and curettage (D and C), 125
Dizziness, 115

E

80–20 Rule, 80, 95–98
Electrocardiogram, 58
Endometrial cancer, 90
Endorphins, 20
Energy level, nutrition and, 79–80
Equipment, 47–52
  for older women, 109
Estrogen therapy, 90
Everest Grand Circle Expedition, 138
Exercise Program charts, 65–72
Exercise tolerance test, 58, 60

F

Fats, dietary, 81–86
Fiber, 86–88
Foot care, 55–56
Foot position for racewalking, 134
Footing, 55
Framingham Heart Study, 17
Friend, walking with, 47

G

Gall bladder surgery, 125
Goal setting, 46–47
Groin stretch, 40

H

Harvard Alumni Study, 16
Head and shoulder position, 27
Health benefits, 14
  lifelong, 16–17
  short-term, 15–16
Heart, 14
  lifelong benefits for, 16
  and short-term conditioning, 15
Heart attacks, 16, 17
  rehabilitation after, 129
Heat stress, 52, 53
High blood pressure, 17
  effect of exercise on, 19
  medications for, 110, 129
  obesity and, 73
  during pregnancy, 113
High density lipoprotein (HDL), 18
Hip and back stretch, 39
Hip motion for racewalking, 135
Hypothermia, 54, 55
Hysterectomy, 125, 129

I

Illness, rehabilitation after, 127
Indoor National Racewalking Championship, 121
Injury, recovery from, 126–27
Iron, 94–95

J

Joints, 14
  degenerative disease of, 73

K

Knee ailments, 127

L

Lancet, The, 121

Lean body weight, loss of, 76–77
Leg stretches, 40, 41
Lower back stretch, 38
Lower leg stretch, 39

M

Madison (Wisconsin) General Hospital, 119
Mall walking, 109
Massachusetts, University of
    Medical Center, 129
    Medical School, 16, 58, 107
Massachusetts, University of Amherst
    Biomechanics Laboratory, 48
    Department of Exercise Science, 58
Medical checkup, 58
Medications, influence on walking of, 110
Mental benefits, 14, 20
Metabolism, 14
    of older women, 108
    resting rate, 76
Modified sit-up, 116, 117
Monounsaturated fats, 81, 84, 85
Motivation, 25, 46–47
Muscles, 14
    short-term conditioning of, 15
    strength and endurance of, 101–5

N

National Geographic Magazine, 141
Neck stretches, 30–33
New England Journal of Medicine, 20
North American Racewalking Foundation, 135
Nutricheck test, 81–83, 86
Nutrition, 79–99
    and calcium, 89–94
    80/20 approach to, 95–98
    energy level and, 79–80
    and fiber, 86–87
    and iron, 94–95
    and osteoporosis, 21, 89–90

and reduction in fat intake, 81–86
and whole grains, 87–89

O

Obesity, 73, 79
  as coronary risk factor, 17
  and high blood pressure, 19
  during pregnancy, 113
  and recovery from illness, 124
Older women, 106–10
Olympics, 132, 133, 136
Orthopedic surgery, 125–26
Orthotics, 127
Osteoporosis, 14, 20–22, 89–90
  in older women, 109
Outside magazine, 142
Overuse injuries, 127

P

Pace, 27
Paffenbarger, Ralph, 16
Pelvic tilt, 116, 117
Personal Walking Log, 147
Physician, clearance for exercising from, 57–58
Posture, 28
Polyunsaturated fats, 81, 84, 85
Powder magazine, 142
Pregnancy, 111–22
  cool-down during, 118
  effects of training during, 112
  exercise guidelines during, 113
  exercise prescription for, 114
  precautions and special considerations during, 118–19
  toning and strengthening exercises during, 116–17
  warm-up during, 115–16
  warning signs and symptoms during, 118
Progress, recording, 47
Pulse, taking your, 45, 60

Q

Quadriceps stretch, 44

R

Racewalking, 105, 121, 130–36
  technique for, 133–35
"Reach for the Sky" stretch, 34
Rehabilitation, 123–29
  cardiac, 127–29
  after injury, 126–27
  after severe illness, 127
  after surgery, 124–26
Reimiller, Doris and Dick, 25
Relative Fitness Level charts, 61
Resting metabolic rate (RMR), 76
Reynolds, Jan, 21, 137–44
Rockport Fitness Walking Test, 58–63, 65, 74
  for older women, 107
  during pregnancy, 114
Rockport Grand Walk Series, 131, 132
Round ligament pain, 118–19

S

Saturated fats, 81, 84, 85
Shin splints, 127
Shoes, 47–50
  and avoidance of injury, 127
  for older women, 109
Short-term conditioning, 15–16
Shoulder stretches, 35
Side stretches, 37, 41
Sit-ups
  diagonal, 116, 117
  modified, 116, 117
Skinfold technique for body fat measurement, 74
Slaney, Mary Decker, 121
Southern Cross Expedition, 139
Sports medicine centers, 127
Spot reduction, 78
Sprains, 126–27
Stomach surgery, 125
Strength training, 101–5
Stress
  as coronary risk factor, 17
  walking to reduce, 20

Stress fractures, 127
Stretching, 29–44
Stride, 27, 28
  for racewalking, 134
Striding events, 47
Stroke, 79
Surfaces, 55
Surgery, rehabilitation after, 124–26
Sweating, 52
Sweetgall, Rob, 52, 55

T

"Target training" zone, 15
Technique, 26–28
  for racewalking, 133–35
Temperature and Humidity Guide, 53
Tendinitis, 127
Testing, 57–63
  frequency of, 66
Thyroid disease, 113
Torellas, Maryanne, 121
Traffic safety, 55
Triceps stretch, 36
Trunk position for racewalking, 134
Twenty-week fitness walking protocols, 67–72

U

U.S. Public Health Service, 125

V

Vaginal surgery, 125
Vaill, Teresa, 132
Vitamins in whole grains, 87

W

Walking Magazine, The, 135
Wall Street Journal, The, 133

Warm-up, 28–29
 and avoidance of injuries, 127
 for pregnant women, 115–16
 for racewalking, 135
 for weight training, 102
Warm-weather precautions, 52–53
 for pregnant women, 118
Weather conditions, 52–55
Weight loss, 14, 25, 73–78
 for adolescents, 22
 for older women, 109
Weight training, 100–105
Wet weather gear, 52
Whole grains, 87–89
Wilkie, Sharon, 100
Wind Chill Index, 54
Wisconsin, University of, 112
World Health Organization, 143, 145

Y

Yeaton, Molley, 106